BLOOMER'S
Developmental
Neuropsychological
Assessments(DNA)

Assessing Basic Executive Learning Processes

Volume III

READING SKILLS
DIAGNOSTIC TEST

Richard H. Bloomer Ed.D., M.S.
Certified Neuropsychlogist
Emeritus Professor
University of Connecticut
Willimantic, Connecticut 06226

Reading Skills Diagnostic Test, (RSDT)
© Brador Publications INC,. , 1957, 1960,1982, 1998

Reading Skills Diagnostic Test - Fifth edition (RSDT)
 © Bloomer's Books 2017
272 Prospect Street
Willimantic CT. 06226

IBSN   978-0-9997244-1-5

Reading Skills, Neuropsychological Assessment, Memory, Phonics, Spelling

"Reading is to the mind what exercise is to the body."
— Joseph Addison

BLOOMER'S
Developmental
Neuropsychological
Assessments(DNA)

Introduction to the DNA series of Volumes

*Until recently, ascribing a particular aspect of behavior to an
unobservable mental process - such as selective attention- removed
the problem from direct experimental analysis. The ability to locate
mental functions to particular regions of the brain whose activities
can be monitored allows even complex cognitive processes to be
studied directly. (Eric Kandel, 1992.)*

Kandel's comment ushered in a new era for psychological assessment. The
focus of neuroscience on the inner workings of the nervous system has
offers an new perspective on assessment of learning problems. The
century old standby's, comparing patients to the "norm" on such global
measures as IQ or Reading Comprehension are fading. Instead of
attempting to squeeze learners into in unruly categories, we have begun
to explore the individual mental processes within the client's nervous
system that contribute to the learning problem. This evolving process
assessment era provides the advantage of allowing the psychologist a
reliable view of the specific executive mechanisms underlying behavior. In
developing Bloomer's DNA I have chosen assessments of those variables
which contribute to the neuro-cognitive processes involved in verbal
learning and memory, with the further advantage that most of these
executive processes respond to specific treatments. The value to the
psychologist in practice of these more reliable measurements is the ability
to isolate specific executive function problems and focus his treatment on
more precise aspects of the learner's difficulty.

Why are we doing this?

Bloomer's Developmental Neuropsychological Assessments (DNA)is a series of mental or cognitive measures designed to probe the executive processes involved in Verbal Learning . It is a sequence of nine tools, designed to determine an individuals facility with significant neuro-cognitive executive processes essential to verbal learning and by inference most school type learning. The DNA battery of tests is a departure from the tests we are accustomed to, which tend to focus on declarative knowledge, such as vocabulary, or facts, or, tests that infer skill level with broad complex processes like reading comprehension.

The DNA tasks parse out known contaminants and systematically select, activate, and evaluate the efficiency of specific neural channels, to reveal the efficiency of simple neuro-cognitive executive process or operation. This approach allows the clinician flexibility, a much more specific diagnosis pattern, and allows development of focused treatment to remediate specific operations or knowledge.

Processing tests are not neural localization tests which point to effected parts of the neural anatomy. The DNA instead seeks to explore the efficiency with which the brain performs certain standard tasks. As such information from the DNA is of great value to anyone attempting to restore or build mental function, and to teachers, especially special education teachers, and rehabilitation therapists charged with improving the performance of children in academic type verbal tasks.

The DNA includes nine volumes. Each of the Nine volumes contains complete separate stand-alone instruments which may be chosen by the psychologist to probe specific executive processes. The Assessments are interrelated to give a complete picture of the client's neuro-cognitive executive functions for verbal learning. Each volume also provides several independent probes of various aspects of the same general theme to provide a more complete picture of the breadth of the client's skills. The scores for these DNA assessments are sufficiently reliable to use for clinical decisions by themselves without resorting to compound or global scores and thus losing specificity of the assessment

A note in passing: I have been following this research thread for some 60 years now. Clearly, I have found the pursuit of neuropsychological assessment variables fascinating. I realize I have only begun to probe the great potential of executive process assessment of human brain. I hope these explorations will stimulate more research and evolve into even deeper probes into the mysteries of processing inf the human brain.

Introduction

All learning rests on three basic executive processing skills:

1. Imitation:

2. Copying:

3. Multiple Discrimination:, the ability to reliably tell one stimulus from another and to act differentially to different stimuli.

Beyond these basics which normally begin to develop at birth or shortly thereafter and progress rapidly at first and gradually more slowly as the brain sheds or inhibits the myriad of possible alternate connections down, to an efficient few that allows us to stabilize behavior within our culture.

By the time a learner reaches school age we have usually determined that these three initial executive processes are in tact. The purpose of schooling is to develop, refine, and enhance a number of additional executive processes which allow the learner to approach and solve more and more complex problems. These processes are sequentially interdependent. That is, is takes a certain level of skill at a lower order component skill in order to recognize and attempt to learn the higher order process.

This set of explorations executive functions is developmental, interdependent, and cumulative in the sense that one must achieve a certain level of mastery of one task before the next task can be successfully performed.

 For example, since stimuli in Short Term Memory fade relatively rapidly. One must achieve a certain level of familiarity and response speed with the stimuli in order to maintain stimuli long enough to be acted upon. By the same token one must have an STM capacity of at least 3 units for learning simple letter/sound correspondences in reading; one for the visual letter, one for the auditory sound, and one for the process of putting them together.

 The DNA focuses sequentially on processes essential to verbal learning in a developmental sequence which reflects the interaction between processing skill and neural development. It is divided into nine volumes. The first eight volumes of the DNA explore eight different areas of cognitive processing.

The several volumes of the DNA are described as follows:

Volume 1. Individual Response Speed: The response speed to a stimulus class is largely dependent upon two factors. The first, the actual experience with the stimulus and the second the structure or the facility of the individual nervous system. The tasks in this volume index that basic speed of neural transmission. Once values for this basic level pf response speed is established, we then may parse out these individual differences in response speed, which allows us to uncover the variables of Persistence, Automaticitry, Arousal Need, and Purposeful Association.

Volume 2. Individual Short Term Memory (STM): STM acts as a gatekeeper to prevent the brain from being overwhelmed by stimulation. The five STM tasks are capacity measures. They provide indexes of the amount or number of stimuli which may be apprehended or acted upon at one time in auditory and visual sequential input channels and in written and verbal output channels . The Volume 2 tasks allow the comparison between input and output channel responding both with and without sequencing. Resting in part on the response speed of the nervous system, and upon the learner's familiarity with the stimuli, STM is a limiting system to control the rate of stimulation that reaches the brain. STM is dependent in part upon the response speed. Since stimuli fade at a rapid rate, a certain minimal level of response speed is required to insert or maintain items in short term memory. Volume 2 also provides us reliable indices of a learner's Impulsivity, Rehearsal Efficiency and Sequencing in Short Term Memory

Volume 3. Basic Reading Skills: The third requisite for progress within our education system is a set of skills and knowledge that comprise at least the bare minimum for independent reading. These include knowledge of the letters and phonemes in the language (a multiple discrimination task), the ability to blend these letter/sounds into understandable words, sufficient capacity to spell short words, and the ability to read those few frequent words that do not follow simple English phonetic patterns. The Reading Skills tasks allow the clinician to accurately determine each learner's missing knowledge, capacities and skills. This allows the pinpoint accuracy for development of specific plans for treatment of each individual learner and results in far superior reading skills.

Volumes 4,5,6. Memory: Once the basic skills have developed the next concern is with long term storage or memory. These tasks represent the intersection between learning and memory. There are two types of memory first described in 338 B.C. by Aristotle . Each type of learning has developed into a philosophical approach to learning and has it's strong adherents.

Natural Memory,
Natural Mamory is often touted by the followers of Jean Jaques Rousseau 'Tabuila Rasa" philosophy. Many adherents to this form of learning feel strongly that it is natural, unfettered, and leads to creativity. Natural memory happens whether you intend or not. Stimulus contiguity is most often random, uncontrolled, and more often leads to myth and superstition followed by cultural degradation. It is fluid, disorganized and much more fun. Natural memory is introspective, responsive to the preceding and to the next stimulus in line, or to the physical/emotional condition of either the surround of the learner, and is often unreliable.

Volume 4. Natural memory (Association) develops without any necessary forethought or intention on the part of the learner to learn. It is the memory of animals in he wild. It's formation, largely pre-vocal, the result of vetting stimuli by the limbic system. Natural memory is primarily a product of interaction with stimuli in the world. The basic main mechanism is stimulus contiguity, the happenstance occurrence of stimuli in the same time and space serves to connect them. In addition to contiguity, stimuli tend to be associated by similarity on one or more dimensions. We use Word Association tasks to probe Natural Memory and extract a Free Spelling Ratio, an Emotional Ratio and a Long Word Ratio to provide the clinician with further information.

.

Artificial Memory
In contrast, Artificial Memory is purposefully placing important events or in memory. Without the stability afforded by of artificial memory human memory would be individual, personal, an sketchy. There would be no History of Mankind , nor any body of collective memories or procedures we could call a Culture. Our knowledge of Artificial Memory reaches back to the pre-historical times of Simonides who first gave us a plan for remembering events and storing them for repetition. Since then many other schemes for enhancing the accuracy of long term recall have been developed. I have chosen to explore two of these Artificial memory enhancement procedures, Serial Learning and Paired Associate learning. Both are highly useful in verbal learning and both have considerable scientific background

Volume 5. Artificial Memory (1) Serial learning, is the purposeful learning of sequences or ordering of stimuli or responses. These sequences aid in recall and allow one to perform tasks with less effort and more accuracy. While serial learning facilitates response chains necessary for efficient responding to more complex materials, the serial skill is the basis of most human complex operations and is a fundamental problem solving skill. The two serial learning tasks provide us with comparisons of Visual/Written with Auditory/Verbal learning , Acquisition Ratio, Seriation, Recall, Retention and Savings and learning set

Volume 6. Artificial Memory -(2): Paired Associate Learning.
Paired Associate learning is forming a deliberate connection between two stimuli. Paired associate learning is the most effective procedure for learning factual materials, Arithmetic, foreign language Vocabulary, Science facts Foreign Language Vocabulary, or any factual material deemed worthy of long term retention. Using Paired Associate learning is much more organized, complete, and rapid, than natural methods.

Purposeful memory is often criticized because it is presumed to require more effort than Natural memory, however artificial memory is a skill in itself. Once developed a learner can become highly proficient. Artificial memory is responsive to systematic learning and repetition and becomes much easier as it is practiced. Artificial memory processes are important for organized stable information important enough to retain for any period of time. In addition practicing these procedures also reinforce the executive functions which make putting things in memory much more facile. The learner with limited skill in these Artificial learning/memory processes is a usually a poor student.

Volume 7 Complex Stimulus processes: Given the severe limitations in the amount of information that may be active in the human brain at any given time, a method of compounding information into simpler bundles is essential for manipulating large quantities of information. The most commonly used method is the development of conceptual hierarchies these are based on grouping stimuli based on a common feature. any items sharing this common feature are grouped into a higher order concept. This allows manipulation and storage of a larger number amount of information in a single instance. This compaction also involves a tremendous loss of information about specific stimuli. In Volume 7 we explore the learner's ability to approach concepts from several differing ways in a series of assessments that probe these higher order processes. Concept Formation, the ability to evolve concepts from exemplars, Concept Production, and Concept Synthesis the ability to evolve a new concept from features of separate stimuli,

Volume 8 Connotative Meaning, Limbic probes; we explore the operations of the amygdala, hippocampus and the limbic stimulus vetting system in this volume. All stimulation must be inmitially processed by the pre-vocal limbic system which vets all stimulation for threat or reward value. We attempt to penetrate into the learner's awareness of the pre-vocal aspects of stimulus processing. We have developed new tools to assess the learner's awareness of word Familiarity, Active/Passive, Strong Weak; Sonic Affect, Emotional Ratio, and Imagery. These novel assessments contribute more than 20 % of the variance in such criterion measures as reading comprehension and probably deserve more attention than they currently draw.

Volume 9 Sharpening Up old Tools. A number of assessment tools in current use hark back a century or more. Many of these have marginal reliability or have the potential to provide us will additional information I have assumed the bravado of altering some of these instruments with a view of making them more useful or more stable. This volume includes several tasks dependent upon the perceptual and tracking abilities of the learner. Modified Gauthier's Bells test by enlarging the test to cover more of the visual field and changed it to increase reliability and to indicate the perceptual search sequence in more normal clients as well as retaining it's original intent to assess hemianopia in stroke and brain damaged individuals We have Modified the Regard Five Point Test, Line Bisection, Trails, Tests A, and B Burtt Letter Maze, Stroop Test, Reverse Spelling to improve scoring and expose values for underlying executive functions.

In summary, The DNA is a wide ranging set of neuo-cognitive assessment tools for in-depth probing an individual learner's executive processing . The DNA provides the clinician with an flexible tool which may be adjusted to meet each learners presenting symptoms. It provides highly reliable scores easily translatable into individual treatment plans focused on the specific process. We provide a method of approaching the poor learner which results in the identification of the specific processes which need treatment., The DNA is particularly useful for those processes used for the manipulation verbal type stimulation found in schools. Application of the DNA to develop specific treatment plans, typically results in increased academic test scores and classroom performance.

Acknowledgments

This work is hardly mine alone. The science of learning and memory reaches back well beyond the recorded history of man. It rests on the work of many scholars and scientists reaching back into antiquity.

Donders, Galton, Ebbinghaus, Weber and Fechner, and Osterman, true exploreres of humam learning science are my immediate precursors. My own explorations of human learning have been marked by wonderful experiences. I was fortunate to have S.D.S. Sprague as a teacher in my very first psychology class. He imprinted the scientific method on my young mind.

At Teachers College, Edward L. Thorndike and Irving Lorge shaped my scientific attitude. Most important was Robert S. Woodworth who never let me forget that there is an "Organism" between the "Stimulus" and the "Response." Percival Symonds provided encouraging mentorship and laboratory space for my early experiments in human learning.

Much credit is due to Irving Lorge who selected me from hundreds of graduate students for his special gruff attention, and weekly thrust upon me, impossible tasks, one after another. One did not fail Dr. Lorge. Irving Lorge was my dragon, whose early demise has left a bewildering emptiness

Even More credit is due Nick Goldberg who opened the mysteries of the nervous system and allowed me to see human functioning in a whole new way.

To my supportive partner, Jan Maya Schold, who gives me the space to think and create and an occasional jog to spur me on. Jan Maya. chipped in many of her precious hours to find and correct my many mistakes .

Within my personal experience. my grandfather Hermon Hutcheson pounded into my wandering pre-adolescent mind his mantra, "There ain't no such word as can't."

Last, and perhaps most important, was my own wicked step mother, Marguerite Barnes Bloomer, who with boundless patience first taught me "how" to learn. She also taught me, that "Learning is not fun." Learning is hard work; it is the accomplishment that is exhilarating, rewarding beyond all else.

BLOOMER'S
Developmental
Neuropsychological
Assessments(DNA)

xiii

BLOOMER'S
Developmental
Neuropsychological
Assessments(DNA)

Preface

Professor Bloomer's Reading Skills Diagnostic Test evolved from my initial study of learning in the 1940's It was spurred by the increasing rate of reading failures in public schools. The effects of teaching masses opf children to learn to read by the 'Whole Word' method were just becoming evident. By that time the poor reader rate reached 30 percent. It became eminently clear that we were doing something wrong with our teaching methodology. Numerous authors offered viable solutions to the problem. Rudolph Flesch, Merrill publishers, The Thorndike-Barnhardt method, and my own Integrated Language Program among others. In spite of their demonstrated superior reading in the classroom, these programs failed to capture the imagination of either educators or major publishers, The problem became how to diagnose and treat the problems of increasing thousands of children who had failed to learn to read well enough to perform in school.

As a psychologist faced with this growing number or poor readers, my attention was drawn ro developing methods for identification of specific problems that lead to straightforward remediation. The common method of supplying a word each time the learner stumbles is both inefficient and non-productive, since it teaches the reader to become dependent upon the tutor. The question I eventually phrased was:

What are the minimum essentials a learner must master in order to become an independent reader who can figure out how to read most words?

Phrased in this way the answers became clear

1. You cannot read if you do not know all the letters of the alphabet in random order.

2. You cannot read if you do not know the sounds as commonly attached to each letter symbol.

3. You cannot learn to read if you cannot hold and connect more than one letter or word in your Short Term Memory at one time.

4. You cannot learn to read if you cannot blend together more than one letter sound into words or part words.

5. You cannot read independently unless you correctly respond to the signals for Long Vowels, Consonant Bigraphs, and Vowel Dipthongs

6. You cannot learn to read Long Vowels, Consonant Bigraphs, and Vowel Dipthongs unless you can hold at least four items in your short term memory

7. You cannot learn to read if you cannot learn by rote those few strange English words that defy our phonetic system.

In essence learning to read requires learning 44 letter/sound combinations and two or three processes, Plus a small bunch of site words. And practice, Practice, and PRACTICE.

Beyond that there is a second question.

What do you mean by learning?

Here again there are a systematic sequence of learning processes to explore the strength of the learning and the method of processing the stimuli.

1. **Recognition**: I show or say the learner a stimulus, and he acknowledges by nodding or otherwise indicating familiarity.

2. **Imitation**: I say a stimulus, and the learner says it back to me.

3. **Copying**: I show a stimulus, and the learner makes a replica of it.

4. **Multiple Discrimination**: I show several stimuli, and the learner indicates the correct one.

5. **Reading**: I show the learner a visual stimulus, and the learner says it back to me.

6. **Dictation**: I say the stimulus, and the learner writes the response.

7. **Recall**: The learner is able to make the response after the passage of time from memory.

Note these tasks are in order of increasing complexity, and performance of each successive level implies success with the preceding levels.

My students and I have used this test for over 50 years. My case reports usually include very specific areas where confusions or weak learning confounds the student. For example:

Johnny has substituted ::

/a/ for /e/ 6 times,	/t/ for /p/ 2 times
/e/ for /a/ 2 times	/s/ for /z/ 2 times
/o/ for /u/ 4 times,	/n/ for /m/ 2 times
/u/ for /o/ 4 times,	
/e/ for /i/ 5 times,	

Or, Johnny failed to blend 2 or three letters into a nonsense syllable 17 times our of 60 chances.

Or, Johnny spelled words of four letters correctly but is unable to spell any word of six letters or longer

Given this type of specific error information the teacher, reading specialist or psychologist can pinpoint their efforts and focus their instruction where it is needed most.

Since this is a developmental teaching test it may be given in parts and the errors in each part remediated before going on to the next section. I have found if I am able to clear up or prevent these and other simple confusions that the learner will progress rapidly in reading, spelling, and language arts in general. The ability to pinpoint the individual learners specific basic problem focuses the remediation on specific learning tasks, and saves pupil and teacher time and effort. I administer the RSDT to nearly all learners who are referred for Reading, Spelling, or Language Problems. I find the results from the the RSDT of much more value to the learner than any standardized normed based reading or intelligence test scores.

RHB.
Willimantic CT.
2017

Teaching Beginning Reading

How do We Teach Beginning Reading?

The reading skill of the learner is heavily dependent upon how the learner is taught. The choice of a curriculum determines what percentage of children will be successful and what the nature or their errors and weaknesses will be.

There are a vast number of methods in use to teach beginning reading to children every few years there a spate of commercial programs expounding some "new" reading teaching program that is presumed to work better, and is less work and more fun for both teachers and pupils. In spite of these attempts over the last 50 or so years the actual reading abilities of children have gone down. Reading tests have been re-standardized downward to compensate for this general loss in reading skill. So we are really unaware of the actual decline in reading ability in the United States.

At present most educators agree that teaching phonics is essential for the beginning readers. The problem arises with defining phonics. What do we mean when we say phonics?

The United States Congress in 1997 realizing the depth of the national reading problem commissioned a NIMH to institute a National Reading Panel to review the reading research literature to answer this question and find the best way to teach beginning reading. The governments of Scotland UK and Australia also independently conducted experimental research studies to answer the question of the best approach to beginning reading. Interestingly all three independent approaches arrived at very similar answers

Methods of Teaching Beginning Reading: Research Findings

The National Institutes of Mental Health convened a panel of experts to study the experimental research to determine what works best in teaching beginning reading. Some of the findings follow:

NIMH/NICHD National Reading Panel

For its review, the panel selected research from the approximately 100,000 reading research studies that have been published since 1966, and another 15,000 that had been published before that time. Because of the large volume of studies, the panel selected only experimental and quasi-experimental studies, and among those considered only studies meeting rigorous scientific standards in reaching its conclusions.

The NIMH panel and the Scotland and Australian experimental studies all concluded that:

1. Systematic Phonics improved children's reading abilities.

2. Guided Oral reading improved learners reading abilities.

3. The effects of Silent reading on learning to read were inconclusive because of lack of sufficient evidence.

4. Other methods were found to be at best neutral or actually inhibited reading growth

Report of the National Reading Panel:
Teaching Children to Read

Phonemic awareness Instruction in phonemic awareness (PA) involves teaching children to focus on and manipulate phonemes in spoken syllables and words (ie.auditory sounds in words but not directly connected to visual letter shapes). It's purpose is to teach children that words are composed of individual sounds.

Skill in phonemic awareness is seen as a precursor to phonics instruction especially for teaching methods which employ the word or larger as a teaching unit and use deconstructive phonics methods. Empirical evidence does not support teaching. Phonemic Awareness except where the unit of teaching is a word, a phrase, or bigger. *If you choose the letter/sound synthesis methods, rather than starting teaching reading by memorizing words, teaching phonemic awareness is a waste of children's time*

Phonics Instructional Approaches Some variety of phonetic training is required for a reader to become independent of a teacher. Generally the NIH phonics methods fall into two major categories:

Deconstructive phonics methods which start with memorizing the Whole <u>word</u> or larger teaching unit and then analyzing, or breaking it apart, it into phonemic components. The student must remember these phonemes and return them in order to reconstruct and then to recognize the product as a word

Constructive phonics methods first teach children the sounds related to specific letters and then shows them to how construct, or synthesize or combine letters or letter/sounds to build words. The teaching unit for these methods is the letter or the letter/sound combination.

Deconstructive phonics: Deconstructive Phonics is a group of phonic related teaching methods which begin with having learners memorize a number of <u>words</u> by the whole word method. Deconstructive Phonics then requires he student to take the new word apart, find the sound relationships to the word parts and then reconstruct the word. To be effective, Deconstructive Phonics requires prior phonemic awareness. Generally the cognitive processing and memory span involved in successful analytic phonic schemes is quite complicated and requires more memory resources. Despite the demonmstrated relative ineffectiveness of the Deconstructive Phonics, they are the most common methods used in U.S. public Schools. The deconstructive phonics methods below are in order from least effective to most effective.

All Deconstructive Analytic Phonics methods have been found by the NICHD panel to be less effective than any Synthetic Phonics method. The panel described four types of deconstructive phonics found in the experimental literature. I have added a fifth, the so-called "combination of methods" which is often commonly extolled in the non-experimental reading literature

1. Embedded Phonics—Teaching students phonics skills by embedding phonics instruction in text reading, a more implicit approach that relies to some extent on incidental learning. Thus when a child cannot guess a word in reading the teacher will give a letter sound Usually the first sound in the word as a hint This is the "first letter and Guess" method This is commonly used in the"Reading is Natural" "Print to Meaning" Whole language methods. Embedded phonics is not really an organized method of teaching phonics at all, and results in the poorest reading of all methods. None the less the method is advocated by some commercial publishers, and there are numerous teachers using this method.

2. Analogy Phonics—Teaching students unfamiliar words by analogy to known words (e.g., recognizing that the rime segment of an unfamiliar word is identical to that of a familiar word, and then blending the known rime with the new word onset, such as reading brick by recognizing that –"ick" is contained in the known word, "kick," or reading "stump" by analogy to "jump"). This method requires considerable mental manipulation and tends to overload the child's memory. Analogy Phonics Has been shown to be very ineffective because of the number of mental steps the child must go through to get the correct word, and is rarely used nowadays

3. Analytic Phonics—Teaching students to analyze letter-sound relations in previously learned words to avoid pronouncing sounds in isolation. This is the method touted by most commercial publishers and is the most common method used in schools. Since it requires deconstructing a word before reconstructing it the short term memory requirements are great and a large number of children cannot master that amount of mental exercise.

4. Phonics through Spelling—Teaching students deconstruct or segment words into groups of phonemes and to select letters for those phonemes the learner must hold each successive phoneme in memory and finally encode, put it all together into the word (i.e., teaching students to spell words phonemically).

5. Combination of methods - Most of the commercial non-experimental literature concerning reading and phonics advocates what is termed a "Combination of methods" wherein the teacher opportunistically uses which ever phonic or other method she feels will be most valuable at the moment. While this varied approach may solve the immediate specific problem, unfortunately long term the learner does not develop a systematic approach for attacking new words independently The use of multiple approaches to word analysis is particularly confusing particularly for bilingual and minority children, if the students themselves do not develop their own systematic approach to unlocking new words.

Constructive Methods is a group of phonic reading methods which begins by teaching <u>letters</u> <u>and/or</u> <u>sounds</u> and then to build, or synthesize, them into words. Synthetic Phonetics involves teaching the alphabetic principle: learning that the graphic letter symbols in our alphabet correspond to speech sounds, and that these symbols and sounds can be blended together to form real words. Word analysis strategies enable students to "sound out" words letter by letter they are unable to recognize by sight. In essence the learner develops a simple pattern for attacking new or unknown words Explicit, direct instruction in phonics has been proven to support beginning reading and spelling growth better than opportunistic attention to phonics while reading, especially for students with suspected reading disabilities (Bloomer, 1963, 1980, Blackman et al., 1984; Chall, 1967, 1983). Beginning readers should be encouraged to decode unfamiliar words as opposed to memorizing them by sight, because it requires attention to every letter in sequence from left to right. This helps to fix the letter patterns in the word in a reader's memory. Eventually, these patterns are recognized instantaneously or automatically and words appear to be recognized holistically (Ehri, 1992; Adams, 1990). Generally the cognitive processing required in synthetic phonics is much simpler than that of any deconstructive phonics method and in experimental comparisons Synthetic Phonics methods constantly produce superior results.

6. Spellers – Teaching children to spell words and part words using letter names in a linear sequential form (eg. C-A-T = cat) through <u>drill</u> <u>and</u> <u>practice</u> allows children to infer phonetic sounds. Children also memorize the syllabarium, basically a two letter consonant-vowel combinations. This is the oldest method of teaching reading and is still one of the best, although slower than other synthetic methods. This includes the Webster's Blue Back Speller and the early McGuffy readers. Spellers are a lot of work for teachers and it is difficult for the child of our digital age to sustain sufficient attention, but it is effective in teaching reading. In languages where the letter name and the sound are the same, (ie. Spanish, French, Italian, etc) these "phonetic" methods are very simple and effective These phonetic spelling methods have been used for two millennia and are very inexpensive to implement.

7. Synthetic Phonics —Learning to read in English is not so simple and the fact that the symbols have names which are different from their sounds complicates the learning problem. Students learn several letter-sound combinations. Usually up to ten maximum by rote and then blend these sounds to form recognizable words. The child then practices making words of the known letter/sound combinations. For Example the child would learn several letter/sound combinations by rote (eg., t, p, a, s) then the child would use these to read several words (eg., tap, at, sat, as, pat, etc.) The child would repeat this with another group of letter/sounds. This is the method adopted after the results of government sponsored experiments by Scotland UK. And is similar to the recent adoption in Australia as the result of their nationwide empirical research studies.

8. Constructive Synthesis Phonetics: potentially has the highest success rate of all phonics systems. Constructive Synthetic Phonetics is divided into two stages. The first stage uses only the Twenty Five Simple Phonetic letter/sounds. The second stage, Complex Phonetics teaches the long vowels, and the other peculiarities of the English language. Success is insured by Introducing the learner to only _one_ single new letter form by its sound at one time. The learner is taught to combine each new letter/sound with the previous learning to construct words, thus rehearsing the previously learned letter/sounds. Constructive phonetics learners read, write and spell every new word they learn. With a good teacher using Constructive Synthetic Phonetics the failure rate is close to zero and children are reading independently within usually three or four months.

It works like this: Before the children are introduced to books or sight words the children begin learning the letters by their sound one at a time. Letter names are not used, only the sound. Children are exposed to a single/letter sound, only the capital form because it is larger and there is less chance of confusing one capital letter with another. Children write as a part of learning every word they read Transition to lower-case comes after the 26 simple letter/sounds have been mastered. Constructive phonics is especially effective with children from low SES backgrounds and bilingual children.

For example: the children will learn the letter 'A' by its sound. The next lesson will teach the letter 'T' by it's sound and begin to construct the word "AT and TAT. The next lesson S sound allows the children to build

AS and SAT.   Teaching the letter M sound allows the learner to construct AM, MAT, MAST, MAM, MASS, and SAM. This also allows the learner to begin to practice sentences SAM SAT AT A MAST   The number of new words increases nearly geometrically with each new letter/sound combination.

Constructive Phonics can be easily taught to non-English speakers by any English speaker who can read. It works equally well with bilinguals and English speakers from low SES backgrounds. It can be used as a rapid transition to English for non-English speakers from any language.

NIMH/NICHD Reading Panel findings and STM Capacity
How are the findings of the NIMH/NICHD panel reflected in the Short term memory of children learning to read? The panel recommended that we begin teaching reading using phonics. Unfortunately, unlike Great Britain or Australia they made no recommendations as to which type of phonics is best. As you have seen phonics covers a wide variety of teaching methods and behaviors, and thus to say teach Phonics is at best a very vague descriptor. However we can delve deeper and shed some light on the choice of type of phonics best suited for a given population. Let us apply our findings concerning Short Term Memory to this problem.

Why are we concerned with this somewhat arcane discussion of these various methods of teaching phonics?
The answer lies in the application of the concepts of Short Term Memory and Response Speed applied to the selection of the teaching stimulus to develop the reading teaching program. The more difficult the beginning stimuli the greater the percentage of children who will fail. Further the more difficult the beginning stimuli the more the impact on minority students, Bilingual and lower socioeconomic children. In essence the selection of a type of reading program will determine not only the percentage of reading failures but to some extent which groups are impacted to the greatest extent. Let us explore this concept further.

STM capacity and type of phonics Instruction
The limiting basis of all learning is the short term memory capacity of the learner. Functional short term memory (STM), or working memory is a representation of the child's immediate memory capacity, the amount of information a child's mind is open to for learning or remembering. The

learner's STM memory size for a given stimulus type controls how much or how rapidly he will learn.

This STM capacity is determined by several variables. STM Capacity is developmental. STM gradually increases up to age twelve or fourteen as the brain matures. This development differs from child to child and from time to time so it is marginally related to intelligence test scores. In essence individual STM for reading via phonics is based on the Familiarity of the learner with the letter/sounds and the synthesis process for putting the letter/sounds together sequentially. The more practice the learner has with the specific stimulation, the more stimulation his mind is open to learning.

Functional memory is also influenced by environmental forces. STM capacity is related to familiarity. STM and memory can be trained to some degree. Unfortunately, memory can as well, be left untrained. Memory is not automatic. It is a neurocognitive process that must be trained and learned and practiced as it is developed. The amount and success of practice tends to expand memory. Thus memory capacity enlarges both developmentally and with practice. The table below shows the average growth of short term memory capacity for grade levels one and two where having sufficient STM capacity is critical for learning to read.

Let's look at some data on STM and extrapolate it the relationship to see the interaction between teaching unit size and children's success in learning to read.

Table 3-1
Functional Short-Term Memory (STM) for single letters and common four letter words, mean and standard deviation by grade level for visual sequential, presentation combined (N=1,128)

Grade Level	N of Pupils	Mean number of **LETTER S** recalled	Standard Deviation letters	Mean number of **WORDS** recalled	Standard Deviation words
Grade 1	138	**3.0**	1.05	**.96**	.6
Grade 2	183	**4.1**	1.33	**1.3**	.9

In essence about half the pupils in first grade will be able to return 3 individual letters and almost one word. By second grade half or these pupils will return about 4 individual letters and about 1.3 words.

Given the Standard Deviation data in Table 3-1, we can calculate the percent of children whose STM will allow then to process stimuli of various sizes. In Table 3-2 we have calculated the percent of children who will correctly respond to stimuli of various sizes. For three letters about 50% of the children will be able to write them from immediate memory. The standard deviation shows us that about 16% of these children will be able to process an additional fourth letter. If you present only two letters about 84% of the children will be able to respond correctly and if you present only one letter at a time 92% will respond correctly.

There is a similar picture for using words as stimuli to teach In Grade 1 A little less that half the students will return a single word correctly. If two words are presented about 9% will respond correctly to a two word phrase and about 3% will respond correctly to a three word phrase. By second grade about 1% will respond correctly to 4 words and 3% will respond correctly to a 3 word stimulus.

Table 3-2
Using Short Term Memory to Predict Number of Children's Correct Answers, Based Stimulus Size and Number in First and Second Grades (N=321)

Letter Stimuli				Four letter Word Stimuli			
Grade1		Grade 2		Grade 1		Grade2	
If you Present	Grade 1 Letters	If you Present	Grade 2 Letters	If you Present	Grade 1 Words	If you Present	Grade 2 Words
Stimuli # of single Letters	Pupil % Correct	Stimuli # of single Letters	Pupil % Correct	Stimuli # of Words (4 letters)	Pupil % Correct	Stimuli # of Words (4 letters)	Pupil % Correct
1	92%	1	99%	1	47%	1	55%
2	84%	2	95%	2	35%	2	42%
3	50%	3	88%	3	17%	3	24%
4	16%	4	50%	4	8%	4	10%
5	8%	5	12%	5	0.3%	5	0.8%
6	3%	6	5%	6	0.01%	6	0.3%

What does all this mean to the child learning to read?

Letters
If we look at our table above, at the end of first grade we would expect the average, about fifty percent of the children to return about three unrelated letters, or units, from memory. The standard deviation shows us that about 16% of these children will be able to process an additional fourth letter. If you present only two letters about 84% of the children will be able to respond correctly and if you select a program which presents only one letter at a time 92% will respond correctly.

The standard deviation of 1.05 tells is that only sixteen percent of the first grade children will return four letters, from immediate memory and about eight percent of first graders will return five letters and only three percent have an STM capacity of six letters.

Number of single letter stimuli is clearly a factor that effects children's learning.

Words

Words are more complex stimuli than letters. The Public Schools currently tend to favor whole word stimulus. About half (forty-six percent) of the first grade children will return one single four letter word from memory. A standard deviation of 0.60 indicates only about thirty-five percent of children, near the end of their first school year, are able to return a more than a single common word from Immediate memory. About 17% of first graders can recall three words from STM and 8% may recall four words..

Interestingly, this 35% unable to return more than a single word at the end of First Grade is near the percent of children who end up in special or remedial education simply because their STM is too limited to grasp what the teacher is attempting to teach. It is these children who are the future reading problems, the anxious, the remedial readers of the future. It is clear the smaller the teaching unit the greater the success rate It is also clear that manipulating teaching unit size can be used as a method of social discrimination. Asking children to learn material which exceeds their memory capacity induces stress, negativism, and deprives them of access to full participation in our society. This STM limitation on reading progress effects children with different cultural backgrounds more severely than middle class children

By second grade about 55% of children will respond correctly to one single word from immediate memory. About 10% will respond correctly to 4 words and 0.03% will respond correctly to a 6 word stimulus. Clearly, the complexity of the stimulation has a even greater effect on children's learning

It is clear from, these STM data that the proportion of learners who succeed on an initial stimulus presentation can be easily controlled by the complexity and the number of stimuli customarily presented to learner's. This limitation can be overcome by additional repetitions of the stimulus but you must bear in mind that the repetitions required increases geometrically with the size or complexity of the stimulus.

What about the curriculum medium (method) chosen to teach beginning reading

The selection of teaching unit size directly impacts memory. The bigger the teaching unit, the greater the complexity of each unit, therefore greater the memory requirement and the smaller the number of learning units the learner can encompass. As the complexity, or size of the teaching unit increases the learner's functional memory capacity decreases and the failure rate increases. This is clear from the table below

These curriculum methods are listed in order of mental processing difficulty from the least complicated to the most. Similarly the effectiveness of the methods in teaching reading goes from bottom to top

Influence of the Curriculum on Reading Success
Learning to read ins an interaction between the child, his abilities and maturation, wth the teacher and the curriculum. The curriculum is a critical factor in the degree of success or failure of learners especially in the beginning phases of reading instruction.

1. **Curriculum** Generally the smaller the teaching unit and the simpler each stimulus the greater the chance s of success

2. **Number of Teaching Units:** The number of items to be learned individually will effect the proportion of students who will succeed or fail. Generally the fewer the different number of overall teaching units in the curriculum the greater the chances of success,

3. **Lesson:** The fewer the number of lessons and less complex the stimuli in a single lesson the greater success.

4. **Speed and repetitions** The more leisurely, the greater the time allotted for each response and the greater the number of repetitions the greater the chances of success.

5. **Rehearsal:** The greater the provision to systematically return anmd rehearse to past learnings the greater the chances of success.

Who Succeeds in Reading

  These factors effect the difficulty of the reading program in turn the difficulty influences the number, or proportion of the children who will be able to pass their state reading basic and proficiency tests The influence of curriculum difficulty is reflected in the race and ethnicity of the learner as well as the functional IQ of the learner. It is the choice of the school's reading methodology and the manner in which it is taught that is a major influence on who is successful.

Functional IQ, Social Discrimination as Determined by the choice of Beginning Reading Teaching Unit***

Unit Chosen for Teaching Reading	Unit Size for Teaching Stimulus	Number of Unique Items for Students to learn	Minimum Functional IQ Required to Learn to Read	Approximate Percent of Students Learning and (not learning) to Read
Single Letters (constructive phonetic or Spelling)	1	26	65	85-97% (3-15%)
Phonic (several letters Synthetic)	1+	44	70	80- 93% (7-20%)
Consonant Vowels (CV)	2	100+	75	77-88% (12-23%)
Syllable (CVC)	3	2100 (520 common)	85	70-85% (15-30%)
Single Words (Sight word reading) most common method	5 - 6	35,000 (600-1000 per year)	95	60- 75% (25-40%)
Phonics (analytic) Most common Phonics	7-12+	Unknown more difficult than words alone	105	52- 67% (33-48%)
Phrases & Sentences "Print to Meaning" **	25+	Unknown	110	45-56% (44-55%)
Paragraphs "Whole language"***	50+	Unknown	115	18-35% (65- 82%)
Story "print to meaning' "**	???	Unknown	120	4-22% (72-96%)

**   Research Studies have shown these methodologies to be <u>destructive</u> to children's ability to read (ie.. less than half the pupils learn to read).

*** Note: research studies have shown approximately 20-30% of children will learn to read with no instruction at all. Further It is likely that 1-3% of school children will not ever learn to read within the tolerance of the public school.

In essence as the table indicates the larger the teaching unit size the fewer children learn to read. It is clear, as the teaching unit size increases, the number of unique items one expects the child to learn increases geometrically and the more functional IQ power or memory capacity required for success. If the learning capacity of the child was infinite, the choice of teaching unit would be a matter of preference. Unfortunately, the six year old beginning reader's brain is far from completely developed and his memory capacity for number of items or size of items is far below what it will be as an adult.

In essence then one can select the percent of failures to learn to read by the selection of a curriculum. It is clear that the increasing number of failures to read, learning disabled children, and numbers of school anxious children who dislike school is more a function of curriculum philosophy than faults in the children themselves. This raises the question as to why empirical evidence of program failure rate should not be required labeling for curriculum packages as they are for drugs.

As it is at present the only criterion for a successful program is it's marketing ability

A Quasi-experimental Test
The following Graphs show the effects over time of beginning reading by Constructive Synthetic Phonetics using a Reading/Typing program as compared with a popular Word method Basal Reader with a Deconstructive Analytic Phonic method series (Bloomer, Cline & Bernazza, 1970). The strongest pupil gains occurred in the disadvantaged children (Bloomer, & Bernazza, 1969)

Table 3-4 shows the a comparison of the two phonics methods in terms of referrals for special or remedial education classes. The dollar value was computed in 1980 dollars

Table 3-4 Special Education Assignment; Constructive Phonics compared with Standard Basal Reader Instruction.

Teaching Program	Number of Pupils	Percent of Pupils Referred to Spec Ed	Number of Referrals per Class (N=25)	Spec ED Cost per Classroom (25 pupils)
Constructive Phonics via Typing	150	11.8%	2.95 (3)	$8,440
Word+Analytic (Basal Reader) Phonics	291	32.4%	8.10 (8)	$23,000

Savings (in 2008 dollars) in special education costs per 25 pupil classroom for Constructive Phonics program is $14,560 ($23.000 vs. $8440). In a school system with 100 classrooms this would amount to a Savings of nearly1.5 million per year, or $582,400 per one thousand pupils, or in 2015 dollars, $1,782,979 per year, per 1000 pupils

Follow up Comparisons
Below are graphic representation of seventh grade follow-up study using the Comprehensive Test of Basic Skills comparing Constructive Phonics in grades 1 and 2 with Analytic Phonics in a Basal Reader Program. Students were randomly assigned to Constructive Phonics Reading Typing Program, or to the Basal reader program for first and second grades

 All students were mixed together at grade 3 and exposed to a standard basal reading program from grades 3 through grade 7. The students were tested in grade three, five and seven using the Comprehensive Test of Basic Skills. The graphs below show the differential progress of students in the standard basal reading program and those who were taught beginning reading by the constructive synthetic method for two years before being placed in standard basal reader classes.

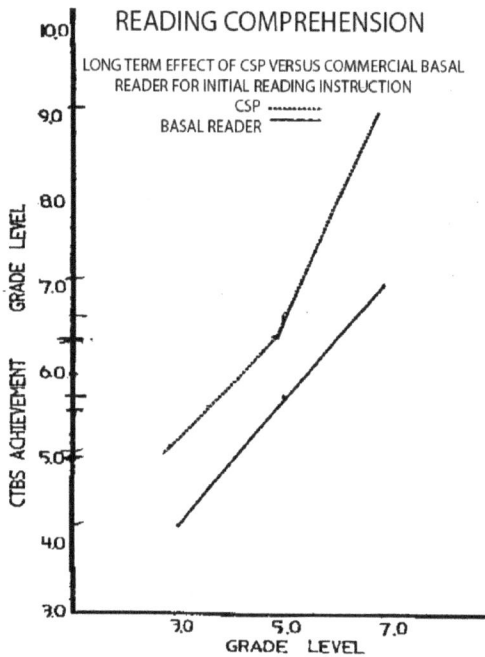

READING COMPREHENSION

LONG TERM EFFECT OF CSP VERSUS COMMERCIAL BASAL
READER FOR INITIAL READING INSTRUCTION
CSP ••••••••••••
BASAL READER ————

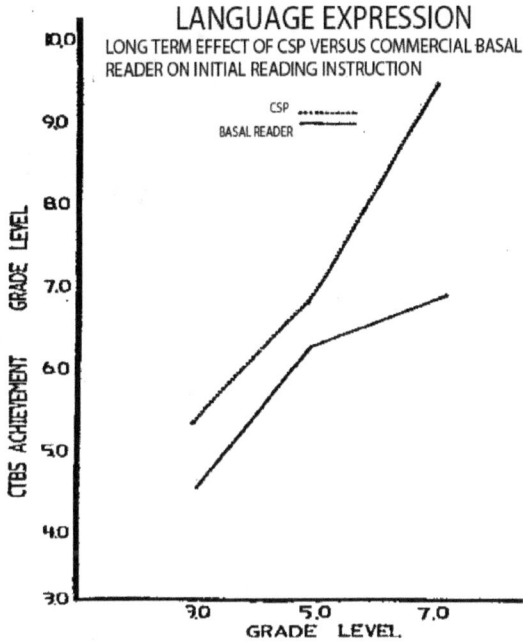

LANGUAGE EXPRESSION
LONG TERM EFFECT OF CSP VERSUS COMMERCIAL BASAL
READER ON INITIAL READING INSTRUCTION

CSP ············
BASAL READER ————

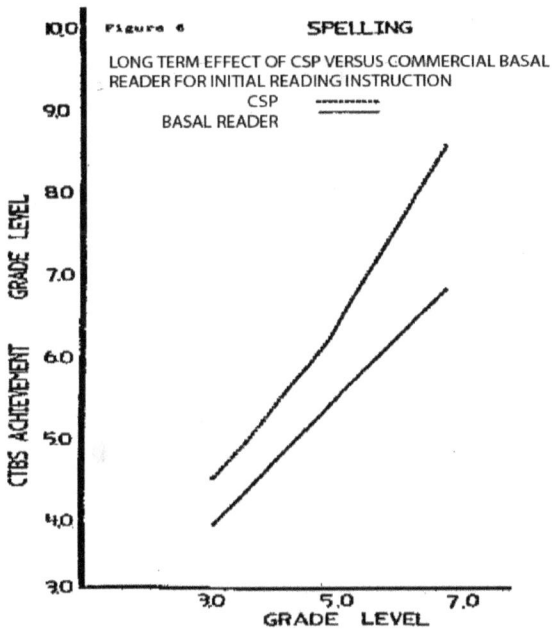

Figure 6   SPELLING

LONG TERM EFFECT OF CSP VERSUS COMMERCIAL BASAL
READER FOR INITIAL READING INSTRUCTION

CSP   ············
BASAL READER ————

BLOOMER'S
Developmental
Neuropsychological
Assessments(DNA)

READING SKILLS DIAGNOSTIC TEST

Reading is, even in our multimedia universe as the gateway to knowledge beyond a learner's personal experience. While educators insist that everyone should learn to read, we are not as often as successful as we should like. Ask ten teachers to describe the best way to teach reading to young learners, you are likely to get ten different answers.

There is probably no more conflicted area in education than divining the proper method of teaching reading. We often rush young learners into books to give the appearance of reading before the basic essentials of reading are mastered. We hear various commentators estimating between 20 percent and 50 percent of school children in the United States fail to learn to read. Nearly all of those youngsters designated as having learning disabilities are not reading up to expectation.

The Reading Skills Diagnostic Test is a "Teaching Test".

 The RSDT probes the minimum essentials for learning to read. It is a test to pinpoint specifics that the learner needs to know to focus teaching on items that will correct his reading difficulties.

The RSDT is not a test to provide a score, a number, a percentile or standard score. It is not a test to compare Johnny or Susy with his neighbors, his class, the state or the nation. It can be used design specific teaching modules to help the learner. It can be used to compare Johnny or Susy's progress toward learning the essential knowledge and processes for effective reading.

The RSDT frees the teacher from the 'lock step' of curriculum and allows you to discover and provide what a learner needs most.

Professor Bloomer's RSDT requires written responses. Spelling a word or a syllable insures the learner can read it and is based on the adage that:

" You can be sure a learner who can spell a word, can read every word they can spell

The RSDT probes the range of knowledge, skills and capacities necessary for independent reading. When the learner has mastered all the tasks from the RSDT he can read books independently with no outside help. All that is required is further practice, practice, practice and vocabulary development. Further, each successive task in beginning reading is dependent upon skill with the preceding task. The RSDT provides a sequential guide to the teacher to teach or remediate a beginning learner to reading independence.

Learning to read requires three things
1. One cannot read without <u>fluent</u> <u>knowledge</u> of each letter in the alphabet connected to its sound.

2. One cannot read without a <u>memory</u> <u>capacity</u> sufficient to hold and process more than one letter at a time.

3. One cannot read without <u>mental</u> <u>blending</u> <u>processes</u> or sequencing to convert visual letters into an auditory sequence to make words.

Independent reading, the ability to read new, unrehearsed material without guidance depends upon the fluent mastery of these simple tasks.

What Knowledge is essential for beginning reading?

1. Content or knowledge   What the reader must know

The new knowledge specific to beginning reading itself is finite and relatively simple to master, if presented carefully in an effective sequence, and with patience.   This letter/phoneme knowledge is essential for converting visual symbols into words

Fluent learning of only 26 letters and 44 letter/sound combinations when taught correctly is well within the grasp of nearly every child. The learner does not have to learn this all at once, but can proceed one letter/sound at a time,
This plus some knowledge of the world allows the learner to make sense of the words he reads. Without this letter/phoneme knowledge and basic cultural experiences the child's reading and subsequent school experience will suffer.

A. **Letters Knowledge**, (Task -1) One cannot read unless the all 26 letters of the alphabet are learned until they are automatic and recognized without thought or puzzlement.

B. **Simple phonetic sounds** (Task -3) One cannot read unless the appropriate sound for each letter or letter combination is fluently automatic.

C. **Complex phonetic sounds** (Tasks -8,9,10) one cannot read unless the appropriate sounds for regular English letter combinations are automatic.

D. **Sight words** Tasks - 11, 12) One cannot read English effectively unless the few irregular English words which defy phonetic synthesis are memorized to an automatic level.

This knowledge is sequential. If knowledge of letter forms is limited, it impinges on learning letter/phoneme combinations. It is not enough to have the learner simply recognize this knowledge or respond to it correctly a time or two. These must become fluently automatic which means there is no intervening thought or puzzlement between the letter and the sound answer or response. Fluent automaticity is only acquired by repetitions rehearsed over time and in a variety of situations.

What memory capacity is required for learning to read?

2. MemoryCapacity in beginning reading

Learning to read requires some memory capacity. Memory capacity is the amount of information that can be held in immediate memory and processed at one time. Memory capacity limits the size of words or sentences a child can readily learn. Each learners memory capacity depends upon the individual learners experience, the fluency of prior learning amount of practice and rate of neural development. Children who have not developed enough memory capacity, who cannot remember several letters/phonemes at one time or employ the mental processes to integrate these letter/phonemes into words or cannot readily learn or remember factual knowledge and will become rustrated and anxious about learning.

1. There are a limited numbers of capacity measures relevant to beginning reading. The memory capacity for letters indicates the learner's potential ability to learn letter/ phoneme combinations. Memory capacity for words is an indicator of the appropriate number of words for sentences in reading material for the specific learner

2. In normal children, these capacities result from interactions between experience, content or knowledge, native ability, learning, processing skill and the learner's age or neural development.

A. **Short term memory (letters)**.(Task -2) One cannot learn to read words if the learner's memory capacity for letters is less than three (3) letter units. Learners can usually remember a greater number of letters than words.

B. **Short term memory (words).** (Task -7) One cannot learn to read simple sentences if the learner's memory capacity for words is less than three (3) word units.

C. **Stimulus length or complexity** (Task -6) The difficulty of material which can be effectively taught to a child is dependent upon its length, complexity, or the number of units presented at one time, and the amount of practice.

Which mental processes are essential for readers?

C. Mental Processes
Third learning to read requires skill at some mental processes, Internal ways of treating visual symbol inputs to convert them into meaningful words. Information is of little value unless your brain knows what to do with it. We call these internal manipulations of facts Neurocognitive processes, or just processes for short. Combining, selecting and ordering are some processes used in beginning reading. If processes are not taught properly, facts or knowledge remain separate and isolated and reading does not become an integrated activity. Word callers and upper grade habitual sounders have not been taught processes.

1. There are a limited number of processes required of a child in beginning reading.

2. Automatic Performance ot these processes is essential to success in beginning reading.

A. **Imitation**. One cannot learn to speak or read if one cannot imitate the names and the sounds of the letters in the language. We will assume Imitation for one cannot talk without imitative skills.

B. **Copying**. One cannot learn to read, write or spell unless one can reproduce visually presented forms of English letters and words. This process is essential for learning to write

C. **Multiple Discrimination**. One cannot learn to speak, write, spell or read if one cannot tell the difference between similar letters and or sounds and if one cannot correctly select the correct letter or sound.

D. **Sequencing** One cannot learn to read without the ability to maintain letter, and word stimuli in the same sequence they are presented.

E. **Synthesis**. (Task- 4,5) One cannot learn to read unless one can blend more than one letter/phoneme sequentially into meaningful words.

F. **Context Clues**.(Task -13) One cannot learn to read effectively of one cannot derive meaning from a sequence of letters or words, which brings us back to the knowledge derived from experience.

The, RSDT is a diagnostic beginning reading test which probes Knowledge fluency which interacts to increase the functional memory capacity of the child to learn and employ the mental processes to unlock new words independently. Since the processes and content in the RSDT are sequential, and require mastery, the total test is rarely given at one sitting. Each task is given one at a time and errors are remediated givint the lraenmer time to mature before going on to the next section of the test. Thus, a test-teach-retest system is recommended. Based upon these premises, the knowledge, memory capacity, and mental processing skills, essential to beginning reading for independent readers:

ADMINISTRATION OF BLOOMER'S

Reading Skills Diagnostic Test

Since the RSDT is a criterion test and we are concerned with mastery, administrative procedures are very important.

Familiarization

Prior to giving any section of the RSDT, the administrator should take a few minutes to become familiar with the specific test and procedures and, if at all possible, should administer that section to a single individual or practice giving the test to a friend until the administrative procedure becomes relatively smooth.

Environment

Environmental conditions are important in all testing and are particularly important in criterion testing. Since we are concerned with each specific error that a child makes as the error becomes the subject for teaching, attempts should be made to reduce distractions in the environment. The testing environment should, therefore, be familiar to the child, that is, children might be tested in their own classroom where distractions are minimal, or in a testing room which is painted in subdued colors and is devoid of pictures, bulletin boards, or other distractions. This will tend to avoid over-identification of the children's problems. Further, if disruptive children are to be found in the classroom, they should be presented the test individually or tested with Level 3 by an evaluator and should not be present during the class group testing. The general rule to be followed is that the environment should not distract the child from the test.

Seating

Since every student's response is important in a mastery model, seating arrangements are particularly important. Children should be seated so that they cannot copy, particularly since the error rate is relatively low on some of the sub-tests and errors are important in planning remediation
. The child who copies one or two correct responses may miss the opportunity for remediation where it is needed and, further, children who copy wrong responses from others might be given additional help unnecessarily. It is often of value to have an aide or a monitor in the room at the time the teacher is giving the test to restrict copying behavior and to make note of copying behavior where it occurs. Children who are habitual copiers should be tested alone.

Manner

Giving the test is a business like procedure and also an important procedure. This is particularly true for criterion tests where we are not concerned with the grade level or other relative measure. Teachers who tend to downplay the importance of a test tend to reduce the focus of the child and he may make more errors than he would if he were somewhat more attentive. Teachers who tend to make light of testing, or to make it humorous, introduce an emotional element which often affects children's scores. The manner of the administrator of the test should, therefore, be very straightforward and efficient. Remember that the purpose of a criterion referenced test is to determine as accurately as possible the child's strengths and weaknesses in order to guide future teaching and remediation.

Voice

Voice and inflection should be as normal as possible. Try to avoid emphasizing certain letters or words by inflection. Instead, make the delivery as flat, even and clear as possible. Children are very attuned to minor changes in an individual's inflection and use these for the purpose of attend- ing or not attending. Using differential inflections for the presentation of test stimuli may produce spurious results.

Directions

The directions for each section of the test should be read verbatim. The reason for this is simple. In paraphrasing directions, test administrators sometimes leave out some critical piece of information which will produce spurious results.

The test administrator should be sure that each child understands the directions. After the directions have been read, if the child does not understand, demonstrate and or paraphrase.

Timing

Timing in a criterion referenced test is very important. This is particularly true for capacity tests. Time limits have been set for each Task. If the teacher moves somewhat more rapidly, children will make errors because the pace becomes frustrating or they will not have time to recall some of the weaker responses. On the other hand, if the time between the items becomes too long, the children become distracted, begin to think of other things, and their mind is off the test. Timing on context tests may be somewhat more flexible since the goal is determination of knowledge and some children may be slow to respond.

It is important to follow these rules for test administration because deviations from standard test administration procedures may produce spurious results which, in turn, would affect the material the child is taught and his future progress in reading.

Scoring:

RSDT is relatively simple to score. By and large, for the content tests and process tests, <u>any error or illegibility is significant</u>. It is true that children may make errors by chance, however, these chance errors are often indicative of a low response strength for the particular material or process. Since we are concerned with a mastery model, it is somewhat better to over-identify than to under-identify. Remediation should take place whenever an error is found, for if an over-identification in a letter or sound does occur, remediation should be fairly simple.

The capacity measures (Tasks 2,6,7), in general, have cutoffs which represent a minimum standard for progress to higher level processing. In general, the capacity measures will indicate to the teacher the amount of material to be taught and/or whether or not the capacity to perform one task is sufficiently great so that the child may readily progress to the next highest order of learning.

Task 1: LETTER WRITING

The rationale for Task -1 is very straightforward. Reading material is composed of letters and, therefore, knowledge of the letters is essential for reading. In general, letters are taught in kindergarten and first grade and generally assumed to be known by the children at subsequent grade levels. Our research has found this not to be the case. In one study, at the end of the first grade only 46% of the children knew all of the letters of the alphabet by dictation, and at the end of the second grade only 65% of the children knew all of the letters of the alphabet. This lack of letter knowledge can be seen to cause some serious problems. Either the child is not focusing on the letters and thus may make errors in reading based upon a partial recognition of the letters in the word, or the child is simply guessing at words which contain letters that he does not know. Fluent knowledge of letter forms is essential for the teaching of phonics. We suspect that some beginning reading techniques like "First letter and Guess" and Whole Language" tend to foster this deficiency and in particular the inability to discriminate between the short vowels where the preponderance of errors are made. Therefore, the letter task at the first testing should be completed to mastery prior to giving the testing phonemes.

Task Objective: To determine letter knowledge and areas for possible remediation.

Task 1: LETTER WRITING

Task Instruction: I am going to say the name of a letter, you print the letter on your answer sheet." Note: Say the number followed by the letter. (Delivery rate, 3 seconds each.)

Task 1: LETTER WRITING

1. b	7. h	12. r	17. x	22. g
2. o	8. k	13. t	18. e	23. a
3. c	9. d	14. f	19. n	24. z
4. m	10. j	15. w	20. u	25. q
5. s	11. l	16. v	21. p	26. i
6. y				

<u>Scoring</u>

Letters are scored either right or wrong. Each error or hesitation is considered significant. If you can't read it's wrong, If there are errors, hesitations or partial letters your learner has not developed letter knowledge skills sufficiently.   It means the letter forms are not sufficiently learned for fluent reading and will interfere with his memory for letters and words and inhibit learning the remaining process of learning to read.

This limited preparation will effect all further attempts at testing or teaching **Stop testing** and develop a remediation plan to correct the deficiencies. Be sure your learner is fluent in letter writing before additional reading testing or teaching is attempted. If your learner has problems at this level it is best ti complete an initial Handwriting progan such as <u>Ptofessor Bloomer's No- Nonsense Handwriting Prgram</u> and return to the RSDT when Your learner has developed sufficient handwriting skill.

Treatment

A consistent handwriting program, preferably teaching manuscript, not cursive, is the best treatment for limited letter knowledge. Using a simple san serif manuscript letter form composed of straight lines and circles that looks like book print is much superior to cursive forms or the more complex serif print. Focus on one letter at a time. Emphasize legibility and practice, returning to the letter at odd times. One major inhibitor to success inn reading is speed. We all seem to be in a hurry, and expose our children to more and more stimulation. When we are teaching reading we must wait for the neural connections to stabilize. If you teach one thing at a time and do it well, your learner will progress more rapidly and without confusion

Treatment. If there are errors in letter knowledge treat these before proceeding. Generally this is a handwriting problem.
　　　　1. Teach one new letter per day.

2. Teach letters that look different on successive days to avoid the confusion of look alikes.

3. Do **not** teach cursive forms, teach print script since it is closer to print it will help learning to read.

4. Teach letter formation one stroke at a time strokes left-top to right bottom.

5. Repeat two or three times and review prior teaching.

6. Review all the letters you have taught daily until automatic do not be fooled into thinking once is enough. It takes time and practice for learning to sink in. Do not be in a rush.

 After you have taught the error letters repeat the Letter Writing Test. If there are errors, RETEACH, When the letters are completely learned go to Level 4 Task 2, Short Term Memory for Letters.

Task 2: SHORT TERM MEMORY: LETTERS

Short Term Memory is a basic capacity task. The Short term memory task is designed to find the number of letters a child can retain for a short period of time.

Letter knowledge and short term memory interact. Solid Fluent letter learning allows a learner to exploit his full short term memory capacity. If the learning of letters is weak, they requires more concentration and effort and short term memory is diminished. Since reading requires matching letters with sounds and combining these letter sounds into words all within the STM system. If Short Term Memory for letters falls below about 3 letters, this processing becomes tenuous and extremely frustrating for the learner. Short term memory is also interactive with learners language experience and age or development. Thus, older learners, up up about age 12 to 14 usually have a somewhat greater short term memory capacity than younger learners.

Task Obiective: To determine the number of letter units the child .can process in memory at one time.

Task 2: SHORT TERM MEMORY: LETTERS

Task Instruction: II I am going to say the name of several letters one at a time. When I finish each one I will say 'write' .You write all the letters you can remember on your answer sheet." (Delivery rate, 2 seconds each letter. Allow about 4 seconds to write the answer.)

Put your Pencils Down.

Now, I will give you two letters. Write as many as you remember.

1.   **J-O-** write
2.   **K-A-** write

Put your Pencils Down.

Now, I will give you three letters. Write as many as you remember.

3.   **B-K-H-** write
4..   **I-P-N-** write

Put your Pencils Down.

Now, I will give you four letters. Write as many as you remember.

5.   **M-V-U-Y-** write
6.   **E-D-M-R-** write

Put your Pencils Down.

Now, I will give you five letters. Write as many as you remember.

7.   **K-R-D-W-O-** write
8.   **U-F-N-Y-V-** write

Put your Pencils Down.

Now, I will give you six letters. Write as many as you remember.

9.   **M-S-L-X-I-K-** write

10.   **A-P-J-Z-C-U-** write

Put your Pencils Down.

Now, I will give you seven letters. Write as many as you remember.

11.   **X-T-Q-J-S-B-R-** write

12.   **O-T-L-G-N-W-Y-** write

<u>Scoring</u>

Short term memory for letters is scored correct if all of the letters at a particular level are correct (i.e., both of the 3 letter sequences or both of the 4 letter sequences, etc.). If you can't read it , it's wrong.   In scoring short term memory, letter order is not significant that is, our concern here is with the number of correct letters reproduced.

 The learner's current "Independent" level is the highest level with all items correct in any order. Since the teachers goal is to improve memory, the teaching level or "Instructional" goal is the number of correct units plus 1.

If the child's short term memory is less than 3 items **Stop further testing**. If the child does not achieve a STM of 3 letters teaching letter/phomeme connections should be undertaken slowly and with great care. The child will need review and drill on the letters themselves to achieve fluency. The best therapy at this point is to teach handwriting of printed letters.

If the child achieves <u>at least STM of 3 letters </u>or more, go to Task-3, Simple Phonics Writing.

What does an error mean.
If your learner makes errors, illegible letters, or hesitations. It means the letter forms are not sufficiently learned for fluent reading and will interfere with his memory for letters and words and inhibit learning the rest of the process of learning to read.

Treatment Short Term Memory for letters is largely dependent upon native skill, maturation, and letter fluency. The teacher has two choices; one is to continue to practice reading and handwriting writing single letters in print form to develop automatic letter fluency. The other is simply to wait until experience and maturation increases the child's short term memory. A combination of both procedures is probably somewhat more useful. Do not be in a rush.

Task 3: SIMPLE PHONEME WRITING

Fluent letter/phoneme relationships are essential to reading. If the learner knows all the phonemes related to each letter, the visual words can be converted to auditory. Then and the brain can process the meaning of the word. Thus, once we have insured ourselves that the child is familiar with the letters and has an adequate short term memory to learn phonics, the next step in the sequence is to insure ourselves that there are no errors in the letter- sound correspondences. The general expectancy in schools seems to be that children will have acquired mastery of simple phonics by the end of grade 2. However, is not always the case. In one study we found over 30% of the children in sixth grade had not achieved mastery of the simple phoneme letter-sound correspondences.

Task Objective: To determine the learner's skill with simple letter-sound relationships and areas for possible remediation.

Task 3: SIMPLE PHONEME WRITING

Task Instruction: I am going to say some sounds, you are to write the letter for each sound as I say it.'
(**Do Not Read Key Words**) (Delivery rate, 2 seconds each. Allow 4 seconds to write the response)

Task 3: SIMPLE PHONEME WRITING

1. /**k**/ (c) as in kick

2. /**y**/ as in yet

3. /**f**/ as in fin

4. /**d**/ as in dog

5. /**u**/ as in nut

6. /**r**/ as in ran

7. /**m**/ as in mad

8. /**s**/ as in sat

9. /**t**/ as in tap

10. /**a**/ as in fat

11. /**i**/ as in insist

12. /**n**/ as in nut

13. /**p**/ as in pot

14. /**w**/ as in wet

15. /**h**/ as in hat

16. /**o**/ as in top

17. /**l**/ as in like

18. /**e**/ as in net

19. /**g**/ as in good

20. /**v**/ as in vest

21. /**k**/ (c) as in cut

22. /**b**/ as in bad

23. /**x**/ as in tax

24. /**z**/ as in zoo

25. /**j**/ as in jet

<u>Scoring</u>

Simple phonics is scored right or wrong. If you can't read it it's wrong. Any single error or hesitation is considered significant and should be subjected to a teaching procedure. It means the letter/phoneme relationships are not sufficiently learned for fluent reading, and will interfere with his memory for letters and words and inhibit learning the rest of the process of learning to read.   Without letter-sound knowledge the learner cannot figure out new words independently and must depend upon techniques like memorizing each word, guessing, or a tutor's help to read. If you are working with a single child who makes any errors **Stop further testing** and train the missing letter/phoneme combinations before proceeding with the remainder of the test, or with teaching word blending.

Treatment

 If you are sure the English letter forms are fluently learned and the STM is at least 3 units the difficulty should lie either in knowledge of phonemes or is the ability to make connections between the form and the phoneme. This is best handled by teachiing a single phoneme to fluency at a time and then adding another and another each as different in sound from each other as possible to reduce any chance of confusion. Remember to review each previously taught phoneme within each lesson to insure they are firmly maintained in memory.

Treatment. If there are errors in letter/sound knowledge treat these before proceeding. Generally this is a problem.

> 1. Teach one new letter/sound per day

> 2. <u>Important:</u> Teach letters/sounds that look and sound different on successive lessons. Use a constructive synthesis method for best results. To Avoid confusion **Do not use** Analytic Phonics programs or those that teach similar phonemes /m/&/n/, /b/&/d/, /f/&/v/, or the short vowels together in single groups.

3. Start with teaching simple forms and short vowels, save digraphs and vowel diphthongs for the future when the short vowels have been mastered. Teach print script only since it is closer to print it will help learning to read Do not teach cursive letter forms.

4. Teach letter formation if need be, one stroke at a time strokes left-top to right bottom.

5. Repeat each letter/sound two or three times and review prior teaching. Each new letter/sound blend previously known letter/sounds with new sounds to make words.

6. Review all the letters you have taught daily until automatic do not be fooled into thinking once is enough. It takes time and practice for learning to sink in. Do not be in a rush.

After you have taught the errors repeat the Phoneme Writing Test, if there are errors, RE-TEACH,

When the learner makes no errors., proceed to Task -4, Open Syllable writing.

Task- 4: OPEN SYLLABLE WRITING

Open Syllable Writing is a blending process task which assesses the child's ability to decode and to synthesize a consonant and a vowel into a whole unit. This simple synthesis process is essential for independent reading. The consonant vowel combinations in task 4 were chosen primarily because they represent the smallest synthetic unit and, therefore, the blending process may be the most clearly seen. This task us also dependent upon the learner's ability to discern the subtle differences between the short vowel sounds

Task Objective: To determine if blending capabilities are sufficient for 2 letter CV blends.

Task- 4: OPEN SYLLABLE WRITING

Task Instructions: I am going to say some two letter sounds, you are to write the two letters that make the sounds. (Delivery rate, 2 seconds each.)

Task- 4: OPEN SYLLABLE WRITING

1. **ja** as in <u>Ja</u>n
2. **pe** as in <u>pe</u>t
3. **to** as in <u>to</u>p
4. **zu** as in <u>zu</u>d
5. **le** as in <u>le</u>t
6. **vo** as in <u>vo</u>x
7. **ga** as in <u>ga</u>s
8. **ni** as in <u>ni</u>t
9. **xa** as in e<u>xa</u>ct
10. **mo** as in <u>mo</u>p

11. **va** as in <u>va</u>st
12. **ho** as in <u>ho</u>t
13. **wi** as in <u>wi</u>t
14. **ro** as in <u>Ro</u>b
15. **cu** as in <u>cu</u>t
16. **lu** as in <u>lu</u>ck
17. **ha** as in <u>ha</u>p
18. **zi** as in <u>zi</u>p
19. **ye** as in <u>ye</u>t
20. **tu** as in <u>tu</u>ck

21. **fi** as in <u>fi</u>t
22. **mu** as in <u>mu</u>st
23. **ba** as in <u>ba</u>d
24. **no** as in <u>no</u>t
25. **si** as in <u>si</u>t
26. **ke** as in <u>ke</u>pt
27. **fe** as in <u>fe</u>n
28. **ri** as in <u>ri</u>sk
29. **de** as in <u>de</u>n
30. **nu** as in <u>nu</u>t

-52-

Scoring

Open syllables are scored as right or wrong. If you can't read it, it's wrong. Any error is considered significant. If your learner makes errors, illegible letters, or hesitations. If there are errors on the Open Syllable Task **Stop Testing**. It means the letter/phoneme relationships, vowel discrimination, blending skill or memory capacity are not sufficiently developed for fluent reading, and will interfere with his memory for to construct letter/sounds into words and inhibit learning the rest of the process of learning to read.

The most common causes for errors in this exercise is vowel confusions. The second most common problem is difficulty with the blending process. It is essential to treat Open Syllable Blending prior to giving Task- 5, Syllable Writing.

Treatment:

Consonant Vowels is an assessment of the learner's ability to blend two sounds. It may be best treated using the Syllabarium Method of Noah Webster where the learner reads and says the two letter sounds separately and then pronounces the combination. The syllabarium is repeted several times a day over several months until the learner becomes fluent at reading and pronouncing. Or hearing and writing the letter pairs This is particularly efficient way to develop vowel discrimination, a major stumbling block to reading for learners whose language is indistinct..Rote practice of a two letter syllabarium both reading aloud and writing from dictation, with attention to clear pronounciation of the short vowels, is often helpful for imprinting the subtle differences in short vowel sounds. Do not be in a rush.

If the child makes no errors go to Task-5, Syllable Writing.

Task- 5: SYLLABLE WRITING

Syllable writing presents a second task of the ability of the synthib blending process. In this case, nonsense syllables are used primarily because meaning- ful words may be in the learner's sight vocabulary and would, therefore, generate spurious results regarding blending or synthesis. Syllable blending is contingent upon the prior four tasks. One cannot blend syllables if one does not know the letters and have established fluent letter-sound
 relationships or does not have sufficient short term memory. Further, one must integrate or synthesize the consonant vowel combinations into single units so the short term memory requirements for syllable writing will be reduced.

If the first 4 tasks have been given and remediated, the probabilities are high that most of the difficulties encountered in task 5, Syllable Writing, will be related either to the blending process or to weak short term memory.

Task Objective: To determine if the phonic blending abilities of the student are sufficient for correct production of 3 letter nonsense words.

Task-5: SYLLABLE WRITING

Task Instruction: "I will say a three letter combination, you write it." (Pronounce the number and the CVC clearly) (Presentation rate, 3 seconds each.)

Task- 5: SYLLABLE WRITING

1. kig	11. tep	21. puz
2. nef	12. rud	22. wum
3. bis	13. wis	23. lof
4. zek	14. jol	24. vis
5. dez	15. fas	25. haj
6. vok	16. yox	26. mip
7. fav	17. rul	27. kov
8. paf	18. hep	28. rus
9. lod	19. kax (cax	29. sim
10. vul	20. lef	30. pab

<u>Scoring</u>

Syllables should be scored as right or wrong. Any error should be considered significant.If your learner makes errors, illegible letters, or hesitations. If any problems arising in task 5, Syllable Writing, **Stop Testing** It means the letter/phoneme relationships, vowel discrimination, blending skill or memory capacity are not sufficiently developed for fluent reading, and will interfere with his memory for letters and words and inhibit learning the rest of the process of learning to read. Look for patterns of errors and select nonsense material to emphasize the blending concept. Pay particular attention to vowel substitutions. Remediation should generally take the form of word a blending exercise.

 Any errors should be dealt with before going on to task 6, Word Length Writing.

Treatment: Syllables (CVC) is an assessment of the learner's ability to blend three sounds It may be best treated using two methods

> 1. The first, Spelling three letter words are presented in lists of about eight words as spelling lessons where the learner will both write the words and spell them aloud from dictation, with attention tp pronunciation of the short vowels, and read them from print, Professor Bloomer's No Nonsense Spelling Program has lists of three letter words

> 2. Rote practice of a three letter syllabarium of Noah Webster, both reading aloud, and writing from dictation where in the learner reads and says the three letter names,(or sounds separately and then pronounces the combination. This may also e reversed and the teacher presents the CVC and the learner says or writes the letters. This is particularly efficient way to develop vowel discrimination. Do not be in a rush.

When no errors are made, go to Task- 6, Word Length: Spelling .

Task 6: WORD LENGTH: SPELLING

Word length Spelling is a memory capacity task designed to help teachers determine how large a unit may be comfortably taught to a pupil. Word length is itself the single most significant variable in predicting word difficulty. If words are too long for the child's memory capacity they will be difficult to learn and induce frustration. Hence, the word size a child may successfully decode and encode is critical to his future reading progress.

From the teacher's point of view, we wish to establish how long a word a child is comfortable learning to guide lesson development to sinure success Since words with complex phonics are generally five or more letters   The cutoff for proceeding to more complex processes is correct spelling of words with 5 letters. This insures sufficient knowledge, memory, and processing skill to deal with more complex encoding/ decoding processes.

Task Objective: To determine an appropriate word length for successful presentation of teaching materials.

Task 6: WORD LENGTH: SPELLING

Task <u>Instruction</u>: "I will say some words. You write them in correct spelling." (Note: Say the numbers. Pronounce the word,. Use the word in a sentence. Repeat the word   Allow 4 seconds for response.)

Two letter	Three letters	Four Letters	Five letters
1. on	5. ant	9. tell	13. plant
2. at	6. win	10. farm	14. trick
3. is	7. rug	11. step	15. first
4. up	8. fix	12. mark	16. storm

Six Letters	Seven Letters	Eight letters	Nine letters
17. dinner	21. blanket	25. millions	29. president
18. kitten	22. present	26. interest	30. apartment
19. temper	23. hundred	27. standard	31. expensive
20. spring	24. careful	28. discover	32. carpenter

<u>Scoring</u>

Word length is a capacity task. The items on the task are scored as right or wrong. If you can't read it, its wrong. The cutoff on the word length is <u>words of 5 letters</u> in length. If the learner fails to achieve an *independent spelling level* at the 5 letter word level, **Stop Testing**. The teacher should develop practice spelling and reading words of four or less letters in length, gradually working up to five letter level and retest with word length spelling before proceeding with more the short term memory for words Task-7.

What the memory assessment shows

- The learner's *independent spelling level* is the one in which **all** four words in a set are spelled correctly. The learner can usually read and spell words of this length correctly. This level is too simple for the learner to benefit from further instruction.

- The learner's instructional spelling level is the one in which the learner makes the first spelling error. You should teach words of this length.

- The learner's *frustration spelling level* is the one in which the learner makes three or four errors in a set. These words are too long for the learner at this time. He will need.

Length of Individual List of Words to Learn

Instructional level	Maximum number of words in list
3 letters	8 words
4 letters	10 words
5 letters	12 words
6 letters	14 words
7 letters	16 words

Treatment

Begin by teaching words at the instructional spelling level in lists.(See table below) Have the learners practice copying words and saying the word and then the letters as they write.

Then practice writing from memory without the word present. Repeat this procedure till all misspelled words can be written rapidly from dictation. Once the frequent words at the Instructional level have been mastered gradually insert words of the next higher length. Continue at least until words of five letters are mastered and then continue testing with Short Term Memory for Words. Professor Bloomer's No Nonsense Spelling Program has spelling words in lists by length in number of letters anf the correct list length The spelling program also presents effective teaching methodology. Do not be in a rush.

T*ask 7: SHORT TERM MEMORY: WORDS

Short Term Memory For Words is a capacity task which will give an indication of the working memory of the child for words of 5 letters in length. The task itself assumes that the child is familiar and can write 5-letter words independently and, therefore, subsumes all of the previous testing.

Task objective: To determine the number of words to be the learner can hold in memory at one time or in a list for teaching purposes.

Task Instruction: I will say two words. When I finish you write them. Do not write until I tell you (Presentation rate, 1 word per 2 seconds. Allow up to 10 seconds for response)

Say: Put your pencils down.

> 1. **after- dress** --(write)
>
> 2. **front- story** --(write)

Say: Put your pencils down.

Say: Now I will give you 3 words. Write as many as you remember.

> 3. **apple- never- build** ---(write)
>
> 4. **until- color- glass** ---(write)

Say: Put your pencils down.

Say: Now I will give you 4 words. Write as many as you remember.

> 5. **black- happy- study- camel** ---(write)
>
> 6. **above- money- visit- robin** ---(write)

Task 7: SHORT TERM MEMORY: WORDS (continued)

Say: Put your pencils down.

Say: Now I will give you 5 words. Write as many as you remember.

    7. **horse- class- sorry- truck- woman** ---(write)

    8. **under- funny- drink- often- block** ---(write)

Say: Put your pencils down.

Say: Now I will give you 6 words. Write as many as you remember.

    9. **every- candy- stand- grass- smart- dirty**---(write)

    10. **carry- stock- order- tramp- bunny- glove**---(write)

Say: Put your pencils down.

Say: Now I will give you 7 words. Write as many as you remember.

    11. **start- uncle- puppy- frost- track- print- muddy** --- (write)

    12. **party- world- angry- stamp- enemy- sport- serve** --- (write)

Scoring

A correct response is all the words in sequence for both trials at a given level correct. If you can't read it, Its wrong. If it's out of order, Its wrong. Short term memory for words equals the number of words where both trials are correct and in order Usually the short term memory for words is less than the short term memory for letters. Short Term Memory as we measured it has two components The first is memory capacity and the second us sequencing. It is patently clear that the child who cannot hold more than one word in his head at one time cannot read sentences with any level of comprehension. Short term memory for words is a good indicator of the average number of words in a sentence that a learner can comfortably read or the number of words in a spelling list to be learned using the table below:

Treatment:: will depend upon whether the problem lies in STM functional capacity or in sequencing.

1. If the learner has progressed to this point an STM capacity problem is either a matter of maturation or lack of automaticity. In this case the old Louella Cole (1937) admonition to" Read, Read, and Read some more." will provide practice for achieving automaticity and also allow time for the maturation processes to evolve.

2. If the problem appears to be sequencing, (correct responses in the incorrect order) it may treated separately. Sequencing and Seriation are aligned processes which are essential for effective problem solving Sequencing is a maturational problem that has a developmental spurt from ages 7 or 8 to about 11 or 12 sequencing is fostered by a wide variety of activities from spelling and counting to memorizing poetry or short prose.

Task 8: COMPLEX PHONICS, LONG VOWELS

All complex phonics are dependent upon awareness of signals that alter the pronunciation of letters or groups of letters. Responding to these signals increases the short term memory requirement for complex phonics. Further, generating an alternative response, (i.e. the long sound rather than the short sound), increases the memory requirement still further.

Task 8 deals primarily with long vowels in their rule or signal situation.

Task Ob.iective: To determine if the long vowel rules have been adequately learned.

(Note: This Sectionis normally done in at least two sittings of 50 words or less each.) If your learner has a reading problem, seems restless or nervous you may cut these sections into smaller chunks and take your time.

Use the STM/List-Lenght chart on page 55 as a guide. You are not in a hurry! Do Not Overload your learner's STM.

Be sure to provide for systematic reviews. Retest and re-teach where necessary

Task 8: COMPLEX PHONICS, LONG VOWELS

Task <u>Instruction:</u> I am going to give you some words one at a time. You write the word I say and spell it correctly."
(Say the number,- give the word,- use it in a sentence,- say the word again) Allow 4-6 seconds for response.

Task 8: COMPLEX PHONICS, LONG VOWELS

1. pay	11. wide	21. tease	31. token	41. stroke
2. few	12. nail	22. roast	32. bugle	42. priest
3. eye	13. suit	23. sewer	33. stripe	43. museum
4. tea	14. hive	24. brain	34. field	44. beside
5. use	15. glow	25. sight	35. trace	45. parade
6. hoe	16. need	26. fruit	36. figure	46. tissue
7. ear	17. team	27. creek	37. bright	47. costume
8. aim	18. tray	28. tribe	38. strain	48. scrape
9. pie	19. glue	29. drove	39. frozen	49. willow
10. owe	20. coal	30. scale	40. creepy	50. polite

Scoring

 The items on the Complex phonics, long vowels task are scored as right or wrong. If you can't read it, its wrong. Either spelling of a homonym is correct. Any error is considered significant. If errors are found in this task, **Stop Testing**. Look for patterns in the errors to determine whether a single long vowel needs remediation and should be subject to repeated practice or remedial teaching, or if the problem lies with any vowel rule. A spelling procedure using words which present the long vowel rule is often successful.

Treatment

There are several long vowel signals which apply across vowels. The learner may have difficulty with one or several of these signals. It is important to treat these signal's separately to avoid confusion. This signal learning should not be attempted with learners who are not automatic with the simple phonic letter sound combinations. It is also much less work for the teacher and the learner to learn the signal than to learn the individual words None of these signals are universal in English. Be sure to avoid those words which do not follow the signal rules to avoid serious confusions.

For instance you might treat vowel - consonant -e (v-c-e) as in "cake" as one signal in all five vowels for several sessions with periodic reviews, before beginning to teach a second signal such as double Vowels as in "need"

Remediate the long vowels prior to going to task 9, the Complex Phonics, Consonant Digraphs.

T

ask 9: COMPLEX PHONICS: CONSONANT DIGRAPHS

Consonant digraphs consist of two consonants which customarily produce a different sound from either of them alone. Fluent knowledge of these deviations is essential for adequate independence in encoding/decoding.

Task objective: To determine if the consonant digraph rules have been adequately learned.

(Note: This Section is normally done in at least two sittings of 50 words or less each.) If your learner has a reading problem, seems restless or nervous you may cut these sections into smaller chunks and take your time.

Use the STM/List Lenght chart on page 55 as a guide. You are not in a hurry! Do Not Overload your learner's STM

Be sure to provide for systematic reviews. Retest and re-teach where necessary

Task 9: COMPLEX PHONICS: CONSONANT DIGRAPHS

Task Instruction: I am going to give you some words one at a time. You write the word I say and spell it correctly."
(Say the number, - give the word, - use it in a sentence, - say the word again) Allow 4-6 seconds for response.

Task 9: COMPLEX PHONICS: CONSONANT DIGRAPHS

1. ash	11. while	21. short	31. starch	41. finish
2. shot	12. shop	22. square	32. throat	42. panther
3. math	13. think	23. chill	33. question	43. quite
4. quit	14. churn	24. whose	34. whether	44. wrench
5. itch	15. quilt	25. north	35. white	45. quiet
6. this	16. month	26. health	36. splash	46. anywhere
7. chip	17. bush	27. church	37. squirrel	47. shovel
8. fish	18. quart	28. squirt	38. length	48. kitchen
9. whip	19. whale	29. wheat	39. whisper	49. thirsty
10. queen	20. lunch	30. fresh	40. chorus	50. whistle

Scoring

Consonant diphthongs are scored for correct items.If you can't read it, it's wrong, If the child makes an error, fluent knowledge of the digraph is suspect. **Stop Testing.** Each item is considered significant and again the tester should look for patterns. Errors may be effectively treated using a spelling procedure with words containing similar consonant digraphs.. Errors in Complex Phonics, Consonant Digraphs should be remediated prior to testing for Complex Phonics, Vowel Diphthongs

Treatment

There are only 5 common Consonant Bigraphs which apply across words. The learner is mostt likely th have trouble with the /th/ bigraph which has two separate sounds. It is best to teach one form thoroughly before attempting the second and with the other learning rthe other consonant bigraphs between the two forms. It is important to treat these diphthong signal's separately to avoid confusion. As with long vowels, Consoant bigraph learning should only be attempted after learners are automatic with the simple phonic letter sound combinations..

Treat Consonant Bigraphs individually. Do not hurry be sure one bigraph is learned well before proceeding to the next. Be sure to provide for systematic reviews. Retest and re-teach where necessary before progressing to Vowel Diphthongs

Task 10: COMPLEX PHONICS: VOWEL DIPHTHONGS .

The vowel diphthongs is the third in the sequence of complex phonics tasks. The material in this task is designed to test whether or not the child uses a second vowel as a cue for alternation in the sound. These pairs of vowels tend to signal a sound different from that of either of the two vowels separately. There are likely to be somewhat more errors in vowel diphthongs than in the other complex phonics tasks. The tester should look for patterns which indicate difficulty with one or another of the vowel diphthongs as they are presented. Complex phonics should be remediated prior to giving task 11, Common Sight Words.

DIRECTIONS

Task objective: To determine if the vowel diphthong rules have been adequately learned.

(Note: This Section is normally done in at least two sittings of 50 words or less each.) If your learner has a reading problem, seems restless or nervous you may cut these sections into smaller chunks and take your time.

Use the STM/List Lenght chart on page 55 as a guide. You are not in a hurry! Do Not Overload your learner's STM

Be sure to provide for systematic reviews. Retest and re-teach where necessary

Task 10: COMPLEX PHONICS: VOWEL DIPHTHONGS .

Task Instruction: SAY- "I am going to give you some words one at a time. You write the word I say and spell it correctly". (Say the number,- give the word,- use it in a sentence,- say the word again) Allow 4-6 seconds for response.

Task 10: COMPLEX PHONICS: VOWEL DIPHTHONGS

1. our	11. hood	21. shoot	31. crowd	41. goodness
2. cook	12. coil	22. enjoy	32. fault	42. point
3. law	13. hawk	23. brook	33. spool	43. ground
4. zoo	14. root	24. found	34. wooden	44. poison
5. joy	15. gown	25. pour	35. oyster	45. maroon
6. poor	16. haul	26. moist	36. choose	46. saucer
7. toy	17. sour	27. broom	37. around	47. powder
8. owl	18. shook	28. awful	38. crook	48. fought
9. hook	19. noise	29. power	39. ought	49. rooster
10. paw	20. hoop	30. football	40. boiler	50. wouldn't

Treatment

There are only 5 common vowel diphthong which apply across words.
The learner may have difficulty with one or several of these signals. It
is important to treat these diphthong signal's separately to avoid
confusion. As with long vowels, and consonant bigraphs, vowel
diphthongs learning should only be attempted after learners are
automatic with the simple phonic letter sound combinations. None of
these signals are universal in English. Be sure to avoid those words
which do not follow the signal rule to avoid serious confusions.

Treat vowel diphthongs individually. Do not hurry be sure one
diphthong is well learned before proceeding to the next. Be sure to
provide for systematic reviews

Task 11: COMMON SIGHT WORDS: WRITING, PART 1

Common Sight Words are basically words which present difficulty when an attempt is made to analyze these words by an encoding/decoding method. None-the-less, these common words are essential for adequate reading and must be taught as sight words through the use of word recognition techniques. Attempts to analyze these words and synthesize them by phonetic techniques will not only prove fruitless but may also act as an inhibitor for phonics. 2The words chosen are basically from the Lorge-Thorndlke's A and AA Words and represent a necessary although not complete list of sight words required for reading. Knowledge of these words may be relatively independent of phonics, but, is dependent upon short term memory and upon the word length capacity variables. These words should be taught by a whole word recognition method prior to the administration of task 12, Context Clues.

Task Objective: To determine the ability to write common sight words that are presented verbally

(Note: This Section is normally done in at least two sittings of 50 words or less each.) If your learner has a reading problem, seems restless or nervous you may cut these sections into smaller chunks and take your time.

Use the STM/List-Lenght chart on page 55 as a guide. You are not in a hurry! Do Not Overload your learner's STM

Be sure to provide for systematic reviews. Retest and re-teach where necessary

Task 11: COMMON SIGHT WORDS: WRITING, PART 1

Task Instruction: III am going to give you some words one at a time. You write the word and spell it correctly.. Allow 4-6 seconds for response.

Task 11: COMMON SIGHT WORDS: WRITING, PART 1

1. so	11. buy	21. hour	31. wear	41. isn't
2. do	12. one	22. baby	32. tear	42. ready
3. he	13. too	23. it's	33. gong	43. knew
4. to	14. off	24. none	34. built	44. guess
5.. my	15. you	25. goes	35. again	45. meant
6. we	16. ache	26. half	36. early	46. sugar
7. any	17. done	27. often	37. know	47. piece
8. are	18. aunt	28. nice	38. touch	48. people
9. Mr.	19. have	29. sure	39. dead	49. cough
10. two	20. Mrs.	30. very	40. chief	50. coming

<u>Scoring</u>
Common sight words are scored right or wrong. Each error is considered significant If the learner makes n error **Stop testing**. Each word should be taught individually. Since the common sight word defies ordinary simple phonetic rules, each item is considered as a separate problem.

Treatment
Sight words tend not to follow the simple rules of phonetics and hence must be treated individually. the test sight words are arranged roughly in order of size to help compensate for short term memory capacity Sight words are best treated as spelling words. <u>Professor Bloomer's No-Nonsense Spelling Program</u> has words ordered by Word length

Be sure to provide for systematic reviews. Retest and re-teach where necessary before progressing to test Context Clues

Task 11: COMMON SIGHT WORDS: WRITING PART 2

Common Sight Words are basically words which present difficulty when an attempt is made to analyze these words by an encoding/decoding method. Nonetheless these words are essential for adequate reading and must be taught as sight words through "the use of word recognition techniques. attempts to analyze these words and synthesize them by phonetic techniques will not only prove fruitless but may also act as an inhibitor for phonics. The words chosen are basically from the Lorge-Thorndike's A and AA Words and represent a necessary although not complete list of sight words required for reading. Knowledge of these words may be relatively independent of phonetics but are dependent upon short term memory and upon the word length capacity variables. These words should be taught by either spelling or a whole word recognition method prior to the administration of task 12t Context Clues.

Task Ob.iective: To determine the ability to read and write common sight words that are presented verbally.

(Note: This Section is normally done in at least two sittings of 50 words or less each.) If your learner has a reading problem, seems restless or nervous you may cut this section into smaller chunks and take your time.

Use the STM/List Lenght chart on page 55 as a guide. You are not in a hurry!   Do Not Overload your learner's STM

Be sure to provide for systematic reviews. Retest and re-teach where necessary

Task 11: COMMON SIGHT WORDS: WRITING PART 2

Task Instruction: "I am going to give you some words one at a time. You write the word I say and spell it correctly." Allow 4-6 seconds for response.

51. cousin	61. making	71. receive	81. all right	91 Wednesday
52. enough	62. ankle	72. thought	82. separate	92. bought
53. fourth	63. caught	73. already	83. stationary	93. together
54. loving	64. brought	74. teacher	84. though	94. kerchief
55. that's	65. haven't	75. through	85. beginning	95. neighbor
56. address	66. January	76. o'clock	86. straight	96. February
57. friend	67. there's	77. trouble	87. couldn't	97. sometime
58. surely	68. believe	78. Tuesday	88. nowadays	98. Saturday
59. I'll	69. instead	79. sincerely	89. remember	99. arithmetic
60. because	70. shoulder	80. weather	90. soldier	100. tomorrow

<u>Scoring</u>
Common sight words are scored right or wrong. Each error is considered significant. Each word should be taught individually by rote. Since the common sight word defies ordinary simple phonetic rules, each item is considered as a separate problem. If the child makes an errort remediate using Spelling procedure

Treatment
Sight words tend not to follow the simple rules of phonetics and hence must be treated individually. the test sight words are arranged roughly in order of size to help compensate for short term memory capacity Sight words are best treated as spelling words. Professor Blooer's No-Nonsense Spelling Program has words ordered by Word length

 (Note: This Section is normally done in at least two sittings of 50 words or less each.) If your learner has a reading problem, seems restless or nervous you may cut this section into smaller chunks and take your time.

Use the STM/List Lenght chart on page 55 as a guide. You are not in a hurry!   Do Not Overload your learner's STM

Be sure to provide for systematic reviews. Retest and re-teach where necessary
When the learner makes no errors, go to Section 12, Context Clues.

Task 12: CONTEXT CLUES

Task 12, Context Clues, is a process task and the only task in RSDT which requires understanding the meaning of words. Fundamentally, for each blank in the task there are a number of possible letters or letter combinations which might make a meaningful word, but only one combination which will make the sentence itself rreaningful. We are testing, therefore, the child's ability to use meaning in and of itself to derive an appropriate word. This is an important skill for independent encoding/decoding and for deriving meaning from content, a major form of vocabulary growth for mature readers. Context clues, as a task, requires considerable short term memory for both letters and words plus an ability to synthesize or blend parts of words together into whole words, as well as a knowledge of letters, phonics and word meanings. It is, therefore, a complex task but one which is very useful to the mature reader.

Task.Objective: To determine the ability to write the missing letters that will complete a word to fit a sentence presented orally.

Scoring Items are scored either right or wrong. If you can't read it it's wrong. If it makes a word, but doesn't make sense, it's wrong. This test probes higher order cognitive procession necessary to develop comprehension and understanding from reading.
Generally you expect a good learner to get most of these correct. Learners who tend to fill in blanks with incorrect words, may tent toward impulsivity. Learners who seem to be able to formulate answers may be lacking in basic experiences or maturity.

Task 12: CONTEXT CLUES

Task Instruction: Each sentence that I will read to you <u>contains</u> <u>one</u> <u>or</u> <u>two</u> words with missing letters. You are to fill in the missing letter or letters as shown by the number of blank spaces in each of the words on your answer sheet.
(Allow 4 seconds for response.) <u>Spell</u> the target word or words in **boldface**. Do not pronounced blanked words.

1. We put money in a __**ank** (b)
2. Did you __**et** my letter? (g)
3. The bird lived in a __**est**. (n)
4. She spread __**am** on our bread. (j)
5. We __**ug** for clams on the shore. (d)
6. The candles were on the __**ake**. (c)
7. Some fruit have __**its** that are hard. (p)
8. He ___**ot** the tiger. (sh)
9. He hit his __**umb** with the hammer. (th)
10. Please take out the ___**ash** for me. (tr)
11. Let's go for a __**ide** in our __**ar**. (r,c)
12. She will __**end** the broken __**ish** with glue. (m,d)
13. I brought a __**ack** of chewing __**um**. (p,g)
14. He __**icked** up the c__t to pet it. (p,a)
15. We study __**aps** in __**lass**. (m,c)
16. The man washed the ___**oor** with a __**op**. (fl,m}
I7. He paid the __**ill** with a ___**eck** .(b ,ch)
18. She sewed the __**em** of her ___**ess**. (h,dr)
19. We have __**un** when we ___**im**. (f, sw)
20. We ___**ink** from a __**up**. (dr,c}
21. He listened ___**en** he heard his mother __**all**. (wh,c)
22. A ___**ip** was docked in the __**ay**. (sh,b)
23. He leaned his ___**in** on his ___**and**. (ch,h)
24. Please ___**ing** the baby to the ___**ib**. (br,cr)
25. The pirate ___**ag** had a __**ull** on it. (fl,sk)

Technical Information

Rather than enter into the debate of how to reach the goal of 100 percent literacy let us analyze basic reading into it minimum necessary components. Reading of language materials requires the conversion of visual symbols into some form of meaning or understanding.

Neurosciense has shown us that reading is a sequential process of continually refining stimulation of retinal cells into letter shapes in the inferior temporal lobe, Checked for familiarity in the amygdala and merged with sounds, from a sound memory store, in the area of the angular gyrus, conbined into words in the tempro-parietal area and associated with stored meanings in the association areas and< remembered and finally into meaning

While this sequence of processes appears to the talented reader to be instantaneous, work with EEG has shown that the process is sequential, that is electrical potential is measured at different times along this route and the process requires nearly 500 msec. The fact that one cannot perceive faster than ones nerves can transmit has made this process appear instantaneous to the layman and has given rise to such reading slogans as "Print to Meaning" and others which have no basis in fact.

RSDT can be used as a classroom test-teach-test method. Thus, some children who might normally be assigned to special education can be remediated within the classroom. Children where ordinary classroom techniques are not effective could be sent to the special educator for short term more concentrated work on specific learnings. A basic goal of the RSDT is to assess thelearners level of content knowledge, process skills and capacity When the chi1d makes no errors on the test, we are insured that the child is capable of performing the basic reading tasks and practice, practice and more practice will help insure great reading in the future

Things You should know about a test

Reliability
1. Can the RSDT be used for school wide assessment to show differences in learning between classes of pupils?

2. Does the RSDT show differences in learning by grade level?.

Validity
3. Do RSDT scores of good readers differ from poor readers?
4. Can you use the RSDT to predict who will be a good reader?

5. Will the RSDT show the effects of treatment?

How well have Eastern Connecticut school children learned their letters?

One of the first essential tasks for American School children learning to read is to learn the English letters. Most educators assume that children have mastered the letters of the alphabet by the end of first grade or by second grade at the very latest. Reading instruction is based upon this assumption. Letter knowledge is assumed to be particularly important for beginning reading because of the traditionally high correlation between letter knowledge and success in reading in first grade. As a .part of a needs study, it was decided to test this assumption of letter knowledge mastery using RSDT test 1, Word Knowledge.

The RSDT Letter Knowledge Test was given 1,290 students from eastern Connecticut in grades 1-6. In the last two weeks of May and the first two weeks in June. Table 1 gives the percent of students who reached the criterion of 100% mastery of 26 English letters and indicates a gradually increasing percent- age up through grade 4 where the percentage seems to stabilize.

As part of the same study, the letter knowledge test was administered to a random sample of 40 students selected from grades 7-11 in a three-county area in Eastern Connecticut. The data indicated that only 73.8% of these students knew all of the letters of the alphabet. This was an unexpected result. The investigators assumed the sample was biased and a second random sample of 41 pupils was drawn from the same population. The results for the second sample were nearly identical.

The conclusion of the study is that the general assumption of mastery of the letters of the alphabet by pupils at higher grades is unwarranted. It is difficult to conceive of an adequate reader who has not mastered identification of the letters, hence, diagnosis and teaching to mastery even such simple subject matters as letter knowledge is important for the learner's progress.

Table 3-5.

Children's Knowledge of English Letters by Grade

Grade	Number of Classes	Number of Learners	Percent Learners All Correct	Percent All Correct Best Class	Percent All Correct Poorest Class	Average Errors Per Learner
1	18	341	41.3	64.3	0.0	5.80
2	22	465	65.9	81.2	0.8	.63
3	6	127	74.8	100.0	47.4	.28
4	3	73	89.0	100.0	25.0	.07
5	5	105	84.8	96.0	0.0	.35
6	4	98	81.7	91.0	20.0	.19
7-11	random students	81	73.8	n.a.	n.a.	.26

Results:

1. By the end of the school year, nearly 59% of first grade students failed to write all 26 letters of the English alphabet from random dictation .

2. More than 34% percent of Eastern Connecticut school students were unable to write all 26 letters of the alphabet by the end of second grade.

3. By the end of third grade 25% of Eastern Connecticut students could still not write all 26 letters of the English Alphabet from random dictation.

Does the RSDT show differences between good and poor readers?

While information about letter knowledge mastery is of interest to educators, it is more important to determine the relationship of Letter/sound knowledge, capacity and processes to reading ability. For this study, a sample of good and poor readers were drawn from the total population of grades 3-6 of a small school in eastern Connecticut. The criterion for selection was students reading a year and one half above grade level for good readers and a year and one half below grade level for poor readers.measured on the Stamford Achievement tests. The sample consisted of 30 poor readers and 42 good readers.

These students were given sub-tests of the RSDT. Means, standard deviations and F ratios are presented in Table 2. All of the means are in the expected direction with the poor students achieving lower scores than the good students. Four of these achieved significance: phonics, consonant vowels, context clues and short term memory for words.

Table 3-6

Reading Skills Diagnostic Test Scores for Good and Poor Readers

RSDT Subtest	Reading Group	Mean	Standard Deviation	F Ratio	1/71 D.F.	Significance
Letter Knowledge	Good	25.42	3.62	3.06		0.085 ns
	Poor	24.57	2.53			
Simple Phoheme Knowledge	Good	21.88	1.90	14.09		0.000**
	Poor	19.80	2.71			
Consonant Vowel Blends	Good	18.50	4.13	9.56		0.003**
	Poor	15.57	3.72			
Complex Phonetics	Good	18.14	7.35	4.25		0.20 ns
	Poor	17.07	6.37			
Context Clues	Good	33.00	4.85	12.69		0.000**
	Poor	26.87	9.91			
STM for Letters	Good	15.90	3.19	4.74		0.095 ns
	Poor	15.37	3.40			
STM for Words	Good	11.38	2.45	22.82		0.000**
	Poor	8.33	2.94			

Does the Short Term Memory of Special Education learners differ from regular class learners?

Comparison of Good and Poor Readers on Capacity and Context Clues Tests

A second group of pupils in a different school in grades 3-6 were given the capacity tests and context clues tests from RSDT. These students were divided into groups on the basis of whether the students were receiving special assistance in reading through Title I or through resource room facilities. Thirty-nine students were in the normal group and 25 students were in the special assistance group. Table 3-7 gives the means, standard deviations and F ratios comparing normals and students receiving special assistance in reading. In this instance, all of the comparisons are significant. The data indicate that elementary pupils reading below grade level or pupils assigned for special assistance in reading, perform more poorly on tests in RSDT III than normal or superior readers.

Table 3-7 Means, Standard Deviations and F Ratios Comparing Normal Third Grade Children (N=39) and Children Receiving Special Assistance in Reading (N=25) on Capacity and Context Clues Tests

Comparison of Third Grade Special Education Students with

Standard Classroom Students

on selected RSDT variables

Variable	Group	Mean	Standard Deviation	F Ratio with 1/62 d.f.	Significance
STM	SpecEd	3.65	.99	7.58	0.008**
Letters	Standard	4.46	.97		
STM	SpecEd	1.62	1.40	16.43	0.0001**
Words	Standard	2.85	1.08		
Word Length	SpecEd	5.24	1.34	6.71	.012*
Spelling	Standard	6.43	2.27		
Context Clues	SpecEd	17.92	9.10	12.80	.0006**
	Standard	27.10	10.75		

* Exceeds the .05 level of Confidence

** Exceeds the .01 level of confidence

*** Exceeds the .001 level of confidence

Can the RSDT Predict who will be a good or poor readers?

Having established that good and poor readers perform differently on various encoding/decoding tasks, the next step is to determine how effective the RSDT is in discriminating good readers from poor readers.

Table 3-8 represents the results of the discriminate function analysis applied to the data in Table 2, indicating the ability of the RSDT to predict good and poor readers. The overall correct predictions were 77.7% and the canonical correlation was equal to .58 indicating that encoding/decoding skills do predict good and poor readers. For this sample, simple phonics knowledge, consonant vowel processing, complex phonics knowledge and short term memory capacity for words were the most important predicting variables. The data confirm our positions that knowledge, process and capacity are all required for adequate reading.

Table 3-8 Percent of Students Correctly Classified as Good or Poor Readers by RSDT II~ Level 4 (N=72)

	Predicted Group		Actual group	
	Poor Readers		Good Readers	
Poor Readers	73%		27%	
Good Readers	18%		82%	

Overall correct prediction = 77.67% Canonical correlation = .58

Intercorrelations of Subtests

The model we are using for encoding/decoding allows several predictions concerning the inter-correlations of subtests. In general, our model would predict that the intergroup correlations of the knowledge, process and capacity sub-tests would be larger than the between group correlations. Secondly, we would predict that since the knowledge, processes, and capacities are hier- archial or sequential, the more complex the knowledge, capacity or process, the higher the correlations. A sample of 161 pupils in grades 3-6 in a small mill town in eastern Connecticut were given sections of the RSDT, Level 4. Table 5 gives the intercorrelations between the RSDT subtests. Most of these correlations are moderate to low indicating some degree of independence between the tests. As may be expected, higher correlations are found between the two processing tests and between the two capacity tests which were given, indicating a tendency for them to be testing more similar material than can be found in intercorrelations between classes of tests. The intercorrelation between context clues and short term memory for words is relatively respectable and indicates, in part, the dependence of context clues upon the short term memory for words.

Table 3-9 Inter-correlation of Reading Skills Grades 3 - 6

Variable	Simple Phonemes	Complex Phonemes	Consonant Vowels	Context Clues	STM Letters	STM Words
Letter Writing	.08	.17*	.09	.27**	.15*	.18*
Simple Phonemics		.29**	.37**	.31**	.11	.29**
Complex Phonics			.35**	.36**	.32**	.40**
ConsonantVowels				.32**	.30	.41**
Context Clues					.30**	.58**
STM Letters						.82**

* $r_{.05}$ w/w 161 d.f. = .15

** $r_{.01}$ w/w 161 d.f. = .21 In general t these predictions are Substantiated by the intercorrelations.

Concurrent Validity

Concurrent validity represents the ability of RSDT to predict scores of other reading tests. Correlation of sub-test scores with other measures of language skills affords two additional predictions from the RSDT model. First, we should expect that the more complex the knowledge capacity or process, the higher would be the correlation with reading comprehension scores; and, second, since the RSDT deals almost exclusively with encoding/decoding skills and very little with meaning and comprehension. we would expect the scores on comprehension bound tests to be considerably lower than dependent more upon encoding/decoding skills. Students in the above sample were also administered the Comprehensive Test of Basic Skills4 which includes measures of reading comprehension, vocabulary, intelligence and spelling.

Table 3-10 gives the inter-correlations of the RSDT with reading, vocabulary, grade level, IQ and spelling as derived from 'test scores from the Comprehensive Test of Basic Skills.. * $r_{.05}$ w/w 161 d.f. = .15 ** $r_{.01}$ w/w 161 d.f. = .21

Reading Skills Related to Achievement and Intelligence

RSDT Variable	Reading	Vocabulary	Spelling	Intelligence	Grade Level
Letter Writing	.22**	.11	.24**	.29**	.11
Phonics Writing	.36**	.13	.33**	.36**	.22**
Consonant Vowel Blend	.43**	.33**	.42**	.37**	.23**
Complex Phonics	.41**	.07	.49**	.42**	.50**
Context Clues	.61**	.37**	.75**	.57**	.46**
Memory for Letters	.28**	.08	.41**	.45**	.31**
Memory for Words	.53**	.20*	.66**	.41**	.49**

As one might expect, RSDT, Level 4 correlates most highly with spelling ability, next with reading, intelligence and grade level, and finally vocabulary. This is to be expected since vocabulary is primarily word recognition meaning. It should also be observed that, in general, the more complex or difficult I the problem generated by the test, the more highly it is correlated with reading, spelling, vocabulary, or grade level, again confirming the model for the sequence of tests in the R~DT III

Table 3-11 gives the multiple correlations of the RSDT with the same criterion variable. As would be anticipated, the RSDT,Level 4 would account for 68% of the variance in spelling, about 47% of the variance in reading, 48% of the variance in IQ and lesser amounts for grade level and for vocabulary. Since vocabulary is much more dependent upon meaning than upon basic encoding/decoding skills, the multiple correlation of RSDT with vocabulary shares only 20% joint variance. On the other hand, the high correlation of vocabulary and meaning (R=.72) and the respectable correlation of RSDT with reading indicates that encodin~/decoding skills account for a substantial portion of the variance in reading comprehension. These data support the notion that RSDT is a valid instrument for prediction of language test scores and, further suggests that it would be a useful tool for differentiating children whose reading problem is encoding/decoding as opposed to understanding or meaning.

Table 3-11 Multiple Correlations of RSDT Level 4 Variables and Reading, Vocabulary, Grade and IQ (N=161)

	Reading	Vocabulary	Grade	IQ	Spelling
R	.682	.469	.641	.692	.826
R	.466	.220	.411	.479	.682
Adj R	.449	.199	.392	.449	.669

Comparison of Knowledge, Capacity , and Process to Reading.

What is the contribution of Knowledge Capacity and process variables to reading?

The data from the above sample of 160 students in grades 3-6 were subjected to stepwise multiple correlation the basic Knowledge variables Letter knowledge and Letter Sound Knowledge produced a multiple correlation (Table3-12) of R = .51 and accounted for approximately 25% of the variance. When short term memory was added to basic knowledge variables, the correlation increased to R = .610 and accounted for approximately 36% of the variance. The addition of consonant -vowel processing variables increased the correlation to R = .68 and accounted for approximately 45% of the variance. Thus, it appears that the basic knowledge he facts of encoding/decoding is not sufficient without capacity and processing skills to account for a reasonable proportion of reading ability grades 3 through-6.

Table 3-12   Multiple Regressions of Phonics Knowledge, Capacity and Processes with Reading

	SimplePhonics & Letter knowledge	Phonics Knowledge+ STM Capacity	Phonics Knowledge + Capacity+ Processes
R	.527	.610	.682
R^2	.257	.372	.466
Adj R^2	.243	.356	.449
Standard error	10.55	9.73	9.00

Applications of RSDT. The following study gives an illustration of the application of RSOT III to a total school population. The site for the present application was a total elementary school in a rural village in Connecticut. Each teacher in the school was asked to list those children who were having difficulties with reading and those children who were not having problems with reading. The whole school was then tested with the Metropolitan Achievement Tests and the Lorge-Thorndike IQ Tests as well as the RSDT   Based upon the teachers estimates and reading scores for the Metropolitan Achievement Test the lowest achievers were selected for a RSDT treatment program.

Subsequent to the pretesting, the pupils in the RSDT Treartment group were assigned to an after school treatment program operating for 40 minutes, 2 days per week for 10 weeks. In this program pupils were assigned depending upon his errors on the RSDT to groups that concentrated upon letter writing, letter/sound combinations, or consonant vowel blending. Thus if a learner made errors in writing letters from dictation his teacher was given a list of the specific letter errors for each child.

When the teacher judged the child has correctly learner all the letters assigned, the learner was retested by an evaluator. If the evaluator found the learner made letter writing errors he was returned to the teacher for additional work on letter writing. If the evaluator found the learner made no letter writing errors he was given a list of his Letter/sound errors and sent to a teacher to be taught the specific letter/sound combinations he missed.

After having corrected their the letter sounds the learner was again evaluated and either returned for more letter/sound instruction or sent to an instructor with a list of missed consonant vowels errors. Each child worked through the after school program at his own pace. There was no work in the treatment plan with regard to context clues or sight words due to time constraints.

Results

Table 3-13 gives a comparison of the experimental and control groups for age, grade and IQ. IQs for the two groups were slightly different, although this difference was not significant. The children selected by the teachers were however, younger and in lower grade levels than the children in the control group.

Table 3-13

Comparison of Demographic Variables Age, Grade and IQ for Demonstration and Standard Teaching Groups for

	Standard Classroom			RSDT Treatment		
	N	MEAN	SD	N	MEAN	SD
Age	117	10.91	2.55	101	9.32	2.19
Grade		4.78	2.32		3.14	1.96
IQ		99.91	11.09		96.67	12.09

Treatment Results, RSDT

Table 10 gives the pre and post test scores on RSDT for both the treatment and control groups. During the 10-week period of treatment the control group made no significant gain in letter identification, lost in ability to do sounds and consonant vowel blends, made no significant increase in sight words and increased significantly in the ability to do context clues.

The treatment group did not improve significantly in letter identification. In part, this, of course, in both instances is due to the fact that almost all the letters were known by both groups initially. The increase in sounds and blends in the treatment group was significant and this was to be expected since this was the area of concentration of the treatment programs. In addition, as a side effect the treatment, groups increased significantly in their ability to read sight words, and, although they did not achieve at the level of the control group, had advanced on the average of about 12 words as measured by the sight word test. In addition, the treatment group increased significantly in their ability to do context clues.

Pre and Post test Scores on RSDT Tests for Standard Classroom Instruction and RSDT Treatment Groups

Table 3 -14 Letter Writing from Dictation

Letter Writing	Standard Classroom			RSDT Treatment		
	N	MEAN	SD	N	MEAN	SD
Pretest	95	24.81	3.88	100	24.46	3.39
Posttest	112	25,22	3.25	100	25.04	2.95
'T'			.088 ns.			1.29 ns.

Table 3-15 Consonant Vowel Blend Writing from Dictation

Blending Open Syllables	Standard Classroom			RSDT Treatment		
	N	MEAN	SD	N	MEAN	SD
Pretest	95	36.05	16.39	100	26.32	14.45
Posttest	112	31.22	14.48	100	38.45	13.94
'T'			2.22**			4.50**

Table 3-16 Writing Sight Words from Dictation

Sight Words	Standard Classroom			RSDT Treatment		
	N	MEAN	SD	N	MEAN	SD
Pretest	95	74.67	43.10	100	36.71	42.76
Posttest	112	75.09	45.45	100	49.06	41.74
'T'			.02 ns.			2.07*

Table 3-17 **Context Clues**

Context Clues	Standard Classroom			RSDT Treatment		
	N	MEAN	SD	N	MEAN	SD
Pretest	95	27.81	13.08	100	2,54	7.76
Posttest	112	18.58	14.05	100	8.79	11.79
'T'			5.65**			4.49**

Since the children were all involved in their regular reading program during the day, these two last significant increases may be seen as an inter-action between the material taught in the RSDT Treatment program and the regular classroom .teaching method. Suffice it to say that the RSDT Treatment group achieved, In the area of context clues, slightly better than the Standard Instruction group performed the pretest. It appears, therefore, that the RSDT Treatment program was successful in increasing the children's abilities to do phonics and i consonant vowel blends and that there was a likely interaction between the treatment program and the regular reading program to assist the children in both sight words and in context clues.

Results, Standardized Achievement

Table 11 gives the pre and post test Metropolitan Achievement Test scores for the experimental and control groups. The control group was approximately on grade level in word knowledge, reading comprehension and spelling at the beginning of the experiment and progressed approximately the expected amount during the 10-week period of the treatment. In no case was the change in test scores significant.

The RSDT treatment group, on the other hand, was approximately one year below grade level at the beginning of the treatment and gained over the 10-week period approximately seven months in word knowledge and in reading comprehension, and approximately eight months in spelling ability. All three of these gains were significant. The study indicates clearly that the use of RSDT in a school situation can be of considerable assistance in the reduction of the number of reading problems in the school .

Table 3-18

Effects of RSDT Treatment on Vocabulary
Compared with Standard Classroom Instruction

RSDT Treatment plus class	Number of Students	Pretest Vocabulary Grade Level	Post Test Vocabulary Grade Level	Gain Vocabulary Grade Level	't' ratio
Mean	99	2.68	3.36	.68 yrs.	3.12**
S. D.		1.43	1.56		

Standard Classroom Instruction	Number of Students	Pretest Vocabulary Grade Level	Post Test Vocabulary Grade Level	Gain Vocabulary Grade Level	't' ratio
Mean	107	4.50	4.70	.20 yrs.	0.62 ns.
S. D.		2.19	2.15		

** $t_{.01}$ = 2.63 w/w 100 d.f.

Table 3-19

Reading Ability: Effects of RSDT Treatment
Compared with Standard Classroom Instruction

RSDT Treatment plus class	Number of Students	Pre Test Reading Grade Level	Post Test Reading Grade Level	Gain Reading Grade Level	't' ratio
	99				3.25**
Mean		2.50	3.19	0.69 yrs.	
S. D.		1.51	1.46		
Standard Classroom Instruction	Number of Students	Pre Test Reading Grade Level	Post Test Reading Grade Level	Gain Reading Grade Level	't' ratio
	107				0.26 ns
Mean		4.30	4.37	0.07 yrs.	
S. D.		2.13	1.95		

** $t_{.01}$ = 2.63 w/w 100 d.f

Table 3-20

Spelling Ability: Effects of RSDT Treatment Compared with Standard Classroom Instruction

	Number of Students	Pre Test Spelling Grade Level	Post Test Spelling Grade Level	Gain Spelling Grade Level	't' ratio
RSDT Treatment plus class					
Mean	99	2.91	3.71	0.80 yrs	3.08**
S. D.		1.54	1.59		
Standard Classroom Instruction	Number of Students	Pre Test Spelling Grade Level	Post Test Spelling Grade Level	Gain Spelling Grade Level	't' ratio
Mean	107	4.77	4.98	0.21 yrs	0.73 ns
S. D.		2.05	2.06		

** $t_{.01}$ = 2.63 w/w 100 d.f

RELIABILITY

.Reliability is clearly as important for a mastery model test as for a norm-referenced instrument. The false/positive results will end in a greater expenditure of teaching time than is necessary and false/negatives produce children who have gaps in their knowledge.

We have presented reliabilities on several samples in two forms. The first, Kuder Richardson Formula 21, is an estimate of the internal consistency of the test. The second form employs Cohen's Kappa, and gives estimates of the number of identical decisions made on odd-even split halves of each test.

Content Tests

Table 12 gives KR-21 reliabilities for three samples, the first being 140 pupils representing the total grade 1 and 2 population of an elementary school in a Connecticut town with a population of 8000. The second sample is 257 pupils (grades 3-6) from a suburban school adjacent to a medium sized city in Connecticut. The third sample of 187 pupils is the total population (grades 3-6) of a rural elementary school in Massachusetts.

Table 3-21

Reading Skills Diagnostic Test Reliabilities
Kuder -Richardson (KR-21)

RSDT Task	Sample 1 Grades 1 - 2 N = 140	Sample 2 Grades 3 - 6 N = 257	Sample 3 Grades 3 - 6 N = 187
Letter Writing	.96	.96	.99
Phonics Writing	.71	.89	.69
Complex Phonics	.78	.98	.87
Word Spelling	.86	na*	na*

*Data is not available, group not tested

The second method for determining reliability is the number or percent of agreement between two forms of the test, or the percent of agreement in an odd-even split. Cohen's Kappa represents an estimate of the percent agreement corrected for an estimate of chance. Cohen has devised two other statistics which reflect on the reliability of the instrument: (1) Kappa Max is the maximum percent of agreement one could hope for from a test corrected for chance; and (2) Kappa/Kappa Max ratio indicates the proportion of the maximum percent agreement in the present testing.

These statistics are presented in Table 3-22 and show that RSDT, is sufficiently reliable for use as a mastery model test.

Table 3 –22
Reliability: Percent of Identical Decisions
Made on Odd-Even Split Half For Content Tests (N=100) Using Cohen's Kappa (Grades 1-6}

	Reading Skills Diagnostic Test Reliabilities Cohen's Kappa, Grades 1-6, (N = 100)			
	Uncorrected % of Correct Decisions	Kappa Corrected for Chance	Kappa/Max Possible Correct Decisions	K/KM
Letter writing	86	39	78	50
Simple Phonics	73	43	73	66
Word Spelling	90	68	100	88

Process Tests

Reliability of the process tests was determined in the same rna~ner as the content tests. Three samples described above were used to determine the KR-21 reliabilities in Table 14.

Is there enough variation in scores to show a difference between learners

Table 3-23
Reliability: (KR-21} for Process Tests for RSDT, Level 4

Test	Grades 1-2 N = 140 Reliability	Grades 3-6 N = 287 Reliability	Grades 3-6 N = 187 Reliability
Consonant Vowel Writing	.78	.86	.72
Consonant Vowel Consonant Writing	.86	.93	n.a*.
Context Clues	n.a*.	.94	n.a.*

* Data not available, group not tested.

Similarly, the percent agreement at the split half of 100 pupils grades 1-6 are presented in Table 15. The reliabilities as determined by percent of identical decisions made on the process test are high enough to allow for relatively accurate prediction of pupils who need remediation in process teaching.

Table 3-24
Reliability: Percent of Identical Decisions Made on Odd-Even Split for Process Tests (N=100) Grades 1-6

	Percent Test Agreement	Cohen's Kappa	Kappa Max Corrected for Chance	K/Kmax Possible Correct Decisions
Consonant Vowel Writing	97	66	66	100
CVC Writing	92	74	74	100

Capacity Tests

Reliability of the capacity tests are measured by Kuder Richardson Formula 21, for a sample of 87 individuals in grades 3-6. The reliabilities are in the middle 60s and low 70s. These reliabilities are restricted somewhat by the number of items and by the manner in which the score is derived. In general, the reliabilities are comparable to the digit span test on the Wechsler tests

Reliabilities of this magnitude indicate that the scores on the capacity tests are primarily useful as a "rule of thumb" estimate of capacity to handle materials that would not in and of themselves be indicative of the general ability of a child as might be determined by an intelligence test. This is even more significant in light of the interaction between knowledge and short term memory in the sense that one must know the content of the short term memory task before short term memory reaches maximum and is, in turn, related to native ability or capacity.

Table 3-25
Reliability (KR-21) for Capacity Tests in RSDT III (N=87)

Test Reliability

STM letters	STM Words	Word Length Spelling
.72	.66	.72

Overal Reliability of Total Test

The total test is rarely given at one setting. However, the user may be curious about the total test reliability. On. 212 elementary pupils given the total RSDT. The overall reliability of the **summed composite score** was r.=.94 using KR-21.   The maximum Validity coefficient for the RSDT is r. = .88 with 12% error variance

Caution The user should be aware that a mastery model instrument has a more restricted variance than a norm-referenced test. Hence, the estimates of reliability using KR-21 tend to be reduced. The reliability estimates reported here may best be interpreted as the lower limit of reliability and the true reliability is probably somewhat higher.

Conclusions:
The Several studies done with the RSDT in school situations indicate:

1. The RSDT has adequate reliability to be used as a Diagnostic instrument of the mastery model variety;

2. The test is useful in discriminating good readers from poor readers;

3. The RSDT is related to reading, comprehension tests, spelling tests and intelligence tests as well as to grade level and vocabulary;

4. Testing for capacity and process as well as content is important in the diagnosis of difficulties in encoding/decoding skills; and,

5. The RSDT , when applied in school treatment situations, the RSDT produces increases in word discrimination ability, in reading comprehension and in spelling ability which are significant.

Table 3-26

Stepwise Multiple Regression Analysis of
Encoding/Decoding Variables with Reading Comprehension*

Variable	Multiple Correlation	Cummulative % of Variance	%Contributed Variance	Simple Correlation	B Weight
Visual STM	.451	20.30	20.30	.451	.510
Consonant Vowel Blend	.492	24.22	3.92	.301	.090
Serial Learning[1]	.503	25.30	1.08	.143	-.095
letter/Sound	.506	25.58	.28	.236	.041
Letter Writing	.509	25.86	.28	.045	-.165

*Sample 1: N=52, grade 3 and grade 5   K = 5.001
[1] Visual STM is a capacity measure from DNA Volume 2 Individual Short Term Memory
  Serial Learning is a Process task from Volume 5 Sequential Memory and Learning

When we explore the components of Reading Comprehension as measured by the CTBS using the serial learning scores and those from the first three volumes of the DNA using Stepwise Multiple Regression, we are able look at the contribution of component skills in the order of their importance to Reading Comprehension. The variables chosen by the Multiple Regression are those primarily related to encoding decoding skills. Clearly the capacity measure Visual STM is dominant in this array, contributing 20% of the variance of reading comprehension. The process variable, Consonant-Vowel blending Is second with nearly 4% of the variance. The serial Learning Process variable adds another 1%.

One might wonder that the additional contribution of Letter Knowledge and Letter sounds is so small, However, since the assessment of Capacity and Processing already requires letter and sound knowledge, most of the variance attributable to those variables is accounted for before the letter sound and shapes entered the equation.

Professor Bloomer's

READING SKILLS

DIAGNOSTIC TEST

Student Answer Form

Richard H. Bloomer Ed.D. DABFE, FACAPP, FACFEI.
Certified Neuropsychlogist
M.S. Clinical Psychopharmacology
University of Connecticut
Willimantic, Connecticut 06226

Task 1: LETTER WRITING

1. _____

2. _____

3. _____

4. _____

5. _____

6. _____

7. _____

8. _____

9. _____

10. _____

11. _____

12. _____

13. _____

14. _____

15. _____

16. _____

17. _____

18. _____

19. _____

20. _____

21. _____

22. _____

23. _____

24. _____

25. _____

26. _____

Task 2: SHORT TERM MEMORY: LETTERS

1. ＿＿ - ＿＿

2. ＿＿ - ＿＿

3. ＿＿ - ＿＿ - ＿＿

4.. ＿＿ - ＿＿ - ＿＿

5. ＿＿ - ＿＿ - ＿＿ - ＿＿

6. ＿＿ - ＿＿ - ＿＿ - ＿＿

7. ＿＿ - ＿＿ - ＿＿ - ＿＿ - ＿＿

8. ＿＿ - ＿＿ - ＿＿ - ＿＿ - ＿＿

9. ＿＿ - ＿＿ - ＿＿ - ＿＿ - ＿＿ - ＿＿

10. ＿＿ - ＿＿ - ＿＿ - ＿＿ - ＿＿ - ＿＿

11. ＿＿ - ＿＿ - ＿＿ - ＿＿ - ＿＿ - ＿＿ - ＿＿

12. ＿＿ - ＿＿ - ＿＿ - ＿＿ - ＿＿ - ＿＿ - ＿＿

Task 3: SIMPLE PHONEME WRITING

1. _____   9. _____   17. _____

2. _____   10. _____   18. _____

3. _____   11. _____   19. _____

4. _____   12. _____   20. _____

5. _____   13. _____   21. _____

6. _____   14. _____   22. _____

7. _____   15. _____   23. _____

8. _____   16. _____   24. _____

                             25. _____

Task- 4: OPEN SYLLABLE WRITING

1. _____

2. _____

3. _____

4. _____

5. _____

6. _____

7. _____

8. _____

9. _____

10. _____

11. _____

12. _____

13. _____

14. _____

15. _____

16. _____

17. _____

18. _____

19. _____

20. _____

21. _____

22. _____

23. _____

24. _____

25. _____

26. _____

27. _____

28. _____

29. _____

30. _____

RSDT Answer form page 5

Task- 5: SYLLABLE WRITING

1. _____

2. _____

3. _____

4. _____

5. _____

6. _____

7. _____

8. _____

9. _____

10. _____

11. _____

12. _____

13. _____

14. _____

15. _____

16. _____

17. _____

18. _____

19. _____

20. _____

21. _____

22. _____

23. _____

24. _____

25. _____

26. _____

27. _____

28. _____

29. _____

30. _____

Task 6: WORD LENGTH: SPELLING

Two letter

1. _____

2. _____

3. _____

4. _____

Three letter

5. _____

6. _____

7. _____

8. _____

Four letter

9. _____

10. _____

11. _____

12. _____

Five letter

13. _____

14. _____

15. _____

16. _____

Six letter

17. _____

18. _____

19. _____

20. _____

Seven letter

21. _____

22. _____

23. _____

24. _____

Eight letter

25. _____

26. _____

27. _____

28. _____

Nine Letter

29. _____

30. _____

31. _____

32. _____

Task 7: SHORT TERM MEMORY: WORDS

2 words- Write as many as you can remember.

1. _____ - _____

2. _____ - _____

3 words. Write as many as you remember.

3. _____ - _____ - _____

4. _____ - _____ - _____

4 words. Write as many as you remember.

5. _____ - _____ - _____ - _____

6. _____ - _____ - _____ - _____

5 words. Write as many as you remember.

7. _____ - _____ - _____ - _____ - _____

8. _____ - _____ - _____ - _____ - _____

6 words. Write as many as you remember.

9. _____ - _____ - _____ - _____ - _____ - _____

10. _____ - _____ - _____ - _____ - _____ - _____

7 words. Write as many as you remember.

11. _____ - _____ - _____ - _____ - _____ - _____ - _____

12. _____ - _____ - _____ - _____ - _____ - _____ - _____

Task 8: COMPLEX PHONICS, LONG VOWELS

1. _____

2. _____

3. _____

4. _____

5. _____

6. _____

7. _____

8. _____

9. _____

10. _____

11. _____

12. _____

13. _____

14. _____

15. _____

16. _____

17. _____

18. _____

19. _____

20. _____

21. _____

22. _____

23. _____

24. _____

25. _____

26. _____

27. _____

28. _____

29. _____

30. _____

31. _____

32. _____

33. _____

34. _____

35. _____

36. _____

37. _____

38. _____

39. _____

40. _____

41. _____

42. _____

43. _____

44. _____

45. _____

46. _____

47. _____

48. _____

49. _____

50. _____

Task 9: COMPLEX PHONICS: CONSONANT DIGRAPHS

1. _____

2. _____

3. _____

4. _____

5. _____

6. _____

7. _____

8. _____

9. _____

10. _____

11. _____

12. _____

13. _____

14. _____

15. _____

16. _____

17. _____

18. _____

19. _____

20. _____

21. _____

22. _____

23. _____

24. _____

25. _____

26. _____

27. _____

28. _____

29. _____

30. _____

31. _____

32. _____

33. _____

34. _____

35. _____

36. _____

37. _____

38. _____

39. _____

30. _____

41. _____

42. _____

43. _____

44. _____

45. _____

46. _____

47. _____

48. _____

49. _____

50. _____

Task 10: COMPLEX PHONICS: VOWEL DIPHTHONGS

1. _____

2. _____

3. _____

4. _____

5. _____

6. _____

7. _____

8. _____

9. _____

10. _____

11. _____

12. _____

13. _____

14. _____

15. _____

16. _____

17. _____

18. _____

19. _____

20. _____

21. _____

22. _____

23. _____

24. _____

25. _____

26. _____

27. _____

28. _____

29. _____

30. _____

31. _____

32. _____

33. _____

34. _____

35. _____

36. _____

37. _____

38. _____

39. _____

40. _____

41. _____

42. _____

43. _____

44. _____

45. _____

46. _____

47. _____

48. _____

49. _____

50. _____

Task 11: COMMON SIGHT WORDS: WRITING, PART 1

1. _____

2. _____

3. _____

4. _____

5. _____

6. _____

7. _____

8. _____

9. _____

10. _____

11. _____

12. _____

13. _____

14. _____

15. _____

16. _____

17. _____

18. _____

19. _____

20. _____

21. _____

22. _____

23. _____

24. _____

25. _____

26. _____

27. _____

28. _____

29. _____

30. _____

31. _____

32. _____

33. _____

34. _____

35. _____

36. _____

37. _____

38. _____

39. _____

40. _____

41. _____

42. _____

43. _____

44. _____

45. _____

46. _____

47. _____

48. _____

49. _____

50. _____

Task 11: COMMON SIGHT WORDS: WRITING PART 2

51. _____

52. _____

53. _____

54. _____

55. _____

56. _____

57. _____

58. _____

59. _____

60. _____

61. _____

62. _____

63. _____

64. _____

65. _____

66. _____

67. _____

68. _____

69. _____

70. _____

71. _____

72. _____

73. _____

74. _____

75. _____

76. _____

77. _____

78. _____

79. _____

80. _____

81. _____

82. _____

83. _____

84. _____

85. _____

86. _____

87. _____

88. _____

89. _____

90. _____

91. _____

92. _____

93. _____

94. _____

95. _____

96. _____

97. _____

98. _____

99. _____

100 _____

Task 12: CONTEXT CLUES

1. We put money in a ___**ank**

2. Did you ___**et** my letter?

3. The bird lived in a ___**est**.

4. She spread ___**am** on our bread.

5. We ___**ug** for clams on the shore.

6. The candles were on the ___**ake**.

7. Some fruit have ___**its** that are hard.

8. He ____**ot** the tiger.

9. He hit his ____**umb** with the hammer.

10. Please take out the ____ **ash** for me.

11. Let's go for a ___**ide** in our ___**ar**.

12. She will ___**end** the broken ___**ish** with glue.

13. I brought a ___**ack** of chewing ___**um**.

14. He ___**icked** up the c___**t** to pet it.

15. We study ___**aps** in ___**lass**.

16. The man washed the ____**oor** with a ___**op**.

17. He paid the ___**ill** with a ____**eck** .

18. She sewed the ___**em** of her ____**ess**.

19. We have ____un when we ____im.

20. We ____ink from a ___up.

21. He listened ____en he heard his mother ___all.

22. A ____ip was docked in the ___ay.

23. He leaned his ____in on his ____and.

24. Please ____ing the baby to the ____ib.

25. The pirate ____ag had a ____ull on it.